ANTONIA WHITE (1899–1980) was born in London and educated at the Convent of the Sacred Heart, Roehampton and St Paul's Girls' School, London. She trained as an actress at the Royal Academy of Dramatic Art, working for her living as a free-lance copywriter and contributing short stories to a variety of magazines. In 1924 she joined the staff of W. S. Crawford as a copywriter, became Assistant Editor of *Life and Letters* in 1928, theatre critic of *Time and Tide* in 1934, and was the Fashion Editor of the *Daily Mirror* and then the *Sunday Pictorial* until the out-break of the Second World War. During the war Antonia White worked first in the BBC and then in the French Section of the Political Intelligence Department of the Foreign Office.

Antonia White published four novels: *Frost in May* (1933), *The Lost Traveller* (1950), *The Sugar House* (1952), and *Beyond The Glass* (1954). This quartet of novels was a major BBC TV serial in 1982. Her other published work includes a volume of short stories, *Strangers* (1954), and an autobiographical account of her reconversion to the Catholic faith, *The Hound and the Falcon* (1965). All these works and *As Once in May*, the early auto-biography of Antonia White, are published by Virago Press, as is the first volume of Antonia White's *Diaries*. Volume II is forth-coming.

Antonia White translated over thirty novels from the French, and was awarded the Clairouin Prize for her first one, Maupassant's *L'ne Vie*, in 1950. She also translated many of the works of Colette. Like Colette, Antonia White was devoted to cats and wrote two books about her own – *Minka and Curdy* (1957) and *Living With Minka and Curdy* (1970). She was married three times and had two daughters and four grandchildren. She lived most of her life in London and died in Sussex, where her father and many generations of her family were born and bred.

Minka
and
Curdy

ANTONIA WHITE

Drawings by
JANET & ANNE JOHNSTONE

Published by VIRAGO PRESS Limited October 1992
20–23 Mandela Street, Camden Town, London NW1 0HQ

First published in Great Britain by The Harvill Press Ltd. 1957
Copyright © Antonia White 1957
This edition offset from The Harvill Press 1957 edition

A CIP catalogue record for this book is available from the British Library

Printed in Great Britain by Cox & Wyman Ltd, Reading, Berkshire

TO MY GODSON
JEREMY FRANCIS ANTONINUS BERTRAM
AND MY GRANDCHILDREN
ANDREW AND CORDELIA CHITTY

I

MRS. BELL felt very sad when her old cat Victoria died. It was true that Victoria had always been rather a severe cat and by no means easy to please. Even when she was pleased, she did not often purr. Victoria did not believe in spoiling human beings; she had strict ideas about keeping them in their proper places. Still, she had been fond of Mrs. Bell in her own way and, provided Mrs. Bell behaved herself and did exactly what Victoria wanted the very moment she wanted it, they had got along very comfortably. Now that Victoria was not there any more, Mrs. Bell found she missed her sulky black-and-white face and the disapproving miaow that said: 'You haven't cut up my fish small enough, come and do it properly *at once*!' or 'How many more times do I have to tell you I don't like my milk straight out of the 'fridge? Come and warm it up this moment!'

Mrs. Bell's flat now seemed very large and empty. It was not really a flat, but the top part of a tall, old-fashioned house, with two floors and an attic as well. Her two daughters were both married and lived abroad and, though she had let two rooms to a charming young girl called Alice, Alice was out at work all day. When Mrs. Silver, who came every morning to clean and tidy up the place, had gone home, the flat was strangely quiet without Victoria's imperious miaow constantly ordering her to open a door or to provide food or entertainment. Even though she was busy writing a book, Mrs. Bell could not help feeling rather lonely.

All her friends were very kind to her and did their best to cheer her up. They came to tea and brought her books to read and flowers to make her rooms gay. And, sooner or later, they always said the same thing:

'You ought to have another cat as soon as possible. A charming, frisky little kitten. Please let me find you one.'

But each time a friend said this, Mrs. Bell shook her head and gave the same answer:

'It is *very* kind of you. But I shall never have another cat. It would be disrespectful to Victoria.'

Her friend Mrs. Black, who was a person who believed in speaking her mind, said:

'Nonsense. I always said you gave in too much to Victoria. Why, she was a perfect tyrant! A nice, affectionate little kitten whom you could train to *your* ways would be much more comfort to you than Victoria ever was.'

Mrs. Bell replied:

'I won't hear a word against Victoria. It is true she had a very firm character and perhaps she *was* rather strict with me. But I am sure it was for my own good. She had very high standards of how human beings should behave towards cats.'

'She certainly had,' said Mrs. Black, with a sniff. 'Pity she had such very *low* standards of how cats should behave towards human beings. I ask you, did she ever thank you for all you did for her?'

'Not in so many purrs perhaps,' admitted Mrs. Bell. 'She thought it beneath her dignity to condescend too much. She did look so very like Queen Victoria, in her black with touches of white, that it was not surprising she really believed she was a queen. In her later years, she preferred to be addressed as Your Majesty.'

'What conceit!' said Mrs. Black, with another sniff. 'When everyone knows she was a grubby little stray cat you took in out of the goodness of your heart. A royal cat indeed! Instead of putting up with her airs and graces you should have reminded her of her humble origin and told her how lucky she was to have such a beautiful home. Good enough for a *really* royal cat . . . a Siamese or a pedigree Persian.'

Mrs. Bell said, quite angrily:

9

'Victoria had a truly regal nature, whatever her origin. If I over-indulged her a little, she deserved it after all the unkindness she must have known as a kitten. And what high-bred cat could have had a finer coat than her glossy black and snowy white? I am proud she adorned my home for so many years and was, on the whole, satisfied with my services. I've never *wanted* a Persian with long hair and a long pedigree.'

She did not, you notice, say: 'I have never wanted a Siamese.' Because this was something Mrs. Bell had never told anyone . . . something she hardly dared to admit to herself. The fact was, that many years ago, just before she had found a grubby, half-starved black-and-white (or rather two shades of dirty grey) kitten shivering on the doorstep, Mrs. Bell had been thinking of buying herself a Siamese. But duty was duty ... and here was a starving, homeless kitten who had been *sent* to her. So what could she do but take it in?

The kitten had grown into a fine plump jet-black cat with a snowy bib and snowy gloves and funny three-cornered white patch on the top of her head that looked like an old-fashioned widow's cap. This black dress with white trimmings, along with the full figure and the imperious, rather prim character she developed while still young, made it obvious her real name could be nothing but Victoria. (At first Mrs. Bell had called her Polly Flinders because the poor little thing had looked as if she had been sitting among the cinders till her coat was covered with ash.) Victoria turned out to be, not only a proud and easily offended cat, but a terribly jealous one. She could not abide so much as the sight of another cat. She seemed to live in constant dread that Mrs. Bell might adopt some other homeless waif. And she was determined no one else was going to share *her* palace.

If another cat dared to put its nose inside Mrs. Bell's flat, Victoria swore at it and cuffed it and chased it away. In the summer, when Mrs. Bell left the windows open, cats from neighbouring houses would often walk along the broad ledge that ran the whole length of the street on the front side and look in at Mrs. Bell and sometimes jump down into her front room. Or they would walk along the roofs at the back of the house and come in through the open window of the bathroom. All they wanted to do was to pay a friendly visit to see what Mrs. Bell's flat was like.

Mrs. Bell would have been only too glad to have a chat with these visiting cats and offer a saucer of milk if the visitor looked as if it felt so inclined. But would Victoria let her? Goodness me, NO. Even if she was sound asleep in another room she seemed to know at once if another cat put so much as a whisker through the window of *her* flat and up she flew to chase it away. Spitting and swearing in a manner most unlike her usual dignified self and putting out long, fierce claws through her spotless white gloves, she routed the boldest intruder. She was even suspicious when Mrs. Bell went out shopping, in case she brought Another Cat back with her. First she looked in the shopping-basket to see if there was Another Cat hidden in it. Then she sniffed Mrs. Bell's coat to find out if Another Cat had rubbed against it. If she found it had . . . which she often did, for Mrs. Bell could never bring herself to be rude to the many cats who spoke to her in the street . . . she was very indignant indeed and stalked away majestically. But the habit of speaking to cats in the street was one thing Victoria had *not* been able to cure Mrs. Bell of doing.

Though she would never have dared to adopt another cat, Mrs. Bell sometimes wondered whether Victoria herself might have been less prim and severe if she had had a companion when she was a kitten, before she was so set in her ways. She might have enjoyed having a friend with whom she could discuss those mysterious cat-secrets that not even the most cat-loving human being can share.

squeek?

What fun the two could have had in that big flat, racing up and down the three flights of stairs, playing hide-and-seek in all those rooms, exploring the attic and playing pranks on Mrs. Bell! Long ago, when her husband was still alive and her married daughters were little girls, they had had two cats, a Russian Blue called Vanya and a sandy-and-white called Fury, who had been brought up together as kittens. They had got up to every kind of mischief together and sometimes quarrelled, but what gay, affectionate cats they had been! And, however much they had teased Mrs. Bell, they had never snubbed or criticised her. Sometimes, when Victoria had been particularly cold and disapproving, Mrs. Bell had wondered whether she herself wouldn't have liked another, less severe cat about the place.

When Mrs. Bell had let her mind stray like this, it had always strayed to one particular kind of cat . . . a cat with smooth cream fur, brown stockings and blue, blue eyes squinting out of a brown face. In fact, to the Siamese she had been longing for before Victoria's arrival. And, now that Victoria was gone, the mere thought of a Siamese seemed so disloyal to her memory that Mrs. Bell had firmly suppressed it. It was the mention of the word Siamese that had made her feel suddenly guilty. And because she felt guilty, she had spoken quite rudely to Mrs. Black.

She said to Mrs. Black, who, though tactless, had meant well:

'I'm very sorry if I sounded rude. But would you

mind if we changed the subject and talked . . . say about hats . . . instead of cats?'

Mrs. Black was only too willing. She much preferred talking about hats to talking about cats. After talking about them very excitedly, she suddenly exclaimed:

'My dear! I've got it! What you *really* need is a new *hat*! Nothing comforts a woman so much! Come out at once and I will buy you one.'

So they went out and Mrs. Black, who was very rich, bought Mrs. Bell a really lovely hat with feathers on it. Mrs. Bell was very pleased and, for a little while, she felt quite cheered up.

2

THE NEXT day, however, Mrs. Bell began to feel depressed again. A new hat is an extremely nice thing to have but you can't wear it all by yourself at home. She put it on a chair in her sitting-room, where she could admire it while she worked. But though it was pretty to look at and pleasant to stroke, it was not much in the way of company. By the time it was four o'clock and time for tea, Mrs. Bell was very glad indeed when her friend Mrs. White dropped in for a cup.

Mrs. White understood Mrs. Bell's feelings much better than Mrs. Black did. Also, she was one of the few people who had understood and appreciated Victoria. Victoria had known this and had always been exceptionally gracious to Mrs. White. So, seeing Mrs. Bell was still far from happy, she did *not* say:

'*Do* stop moping about Victoria.'

Instead, she said tactfully:

'What a beautiful new hat I see on that chair. I hope it makes you feel a *little* happier.'

'Not quite as much as I could wish,' said Mrs. Bell with

a sigh. Then, because she could say things to Mrs. White
that she could never say to Mrs. Black, she went on:

'It *is* a beautiful hat. Yet, even that *reminds* me. Once
I could never have left that beautiful hat lying about on a
chair. *She* would have sat on it at once and squashed it all
out of shape. Or pulled out the feathers, thinking it was
a bird.'

'Yes, indeed,' said Mrs. White sympathetically. And
they both drank a cup of tea in respectful silence. Then
Mrs. White said gently:

'It should be some comfort to you to realise that no cat
could have had a longer and pleasanter life. Please don't
be cross with me if I say I'm sorry you are so determined
never to have another. It seems so hard to think that
some deserving kitten, perhaps longing at this very moment for a home, with all comforts and first-class service,
may never find one as good as this.'

'I *have* thought of that,' admitted Mrs. Bell. 'But even when I have got over her loss a little, I do not feel it would be right. Certainly not for a long, long time. I must pay tribute to her memory.'

'Certainly,' said Mrs. White. 'And it is precisely as a tribute to her memory that I think you ought to adopt another cat.'

Mrs. Bell asked, in surprise:

'Whatever do you mean?'

'Listen. Didn't Victoria spend all the long years of her reign here training you to be an ideal cat-hostess?'

'Yes, indeed. She spared herself no pains in my education. None of my cats has ever taught me as much as she did.'

'Exactly. And do you honestly think that Victoria would want to have all her hard work wasted? Surely her true object was to raise the status of all cats and secure better living conditions for them?'

'I fear not,' said Mrs. Bell. 'She trained me to *her* exclusive personal service. Alas, far from wishing to promote the welfare of cats in general, Victoria despised and detested her own race.'

'I think,' said Mrs. White, 'that was due to her jealous, if not demonstrative, devotion to you.'

'She did care for me in her own way,' said Mrs. Bell, 'whatever impression she often gave to the contrary. I was always so glad you appreciated the sterling qualities under that somewhat forbidding manner.'

17

'I fear few did,' said Mrs. White. 'Which is why you must do all you can to preserve her reputation from being defamed.'

'Surely you do not imagine I would ever speak ill of Victoria?'

'Of course not,' said Mrs. White soothingly. 'But, without meaning to, you might cause others to do so. Suppose spiteful rumours began to circulate.'

'*What* rumours?'

'Use your imagination. "My dear, isn't it peculiar that Mrs. Bell, who was always so devoted to cats, swears she'll never have another?" "You mean you haven't heard? My dear, Victoria was such a *tyrant* and made Mrs. Bell's life such a misery, it's put her off cats for life!"'

'Could people really say such wicked things?' gasped Mrs. Bell.

'I fear so. But there is one way to silence scandalous tongues. And that is . . . after a suitable interval, of course . . .'

'Adopt a new kitten?' whispered Mrs. Bell.

Mrs. White nodded.

'After all, what could be better proof of the great joy and comfort Victoria was to you? If people see you can no longer *live* without a cat, they will forget all their criticisms of her and speak nothing but good of her late Majesty.'

'You have given me new and grave reasons,' said Mrs.

Bell. 'All the same, I do not feel equal to making so great a decision yet.'

'Of course not,' said Mrs. White, as she stood up to go. 'But, I implore you, do think over all that I have said.'

3

WHEN MRS. WHITE had gone, Mrs. Bell *did* think over all her friend had said. She thought it over very carefully. She did not get as far as deciding to have another cat of her own. What she did decide was to be extra nice to all the cats she met in the street.

She said to herself: 'That will get over all Mrs. White's objections while leaving my home sacred to the memory of Victoria. I shall not forget the many variations of stroking she taught me if I practise them on others. I shall also keep up my cat-language, which is now quite fluent though my accent will never be perfect. Best of all, people will realise that my life with Victoria has given me increased respect and affection for the entire race of cats.'

The very next day, she began to carry out her plan. She found it a definite comfort. Though her flat still seemed very large and lonely, her walks became something to look forward to. And, when she got home, she would think about the various cats she had met and compare their characters.

In a very short time, many cats who had formerly been mere acquaintances became well-known friends. There was Micky, the one-eared tabby Tom who always sat on the same post of the fence round the square. She had to be careful with Micky. Morning after morning, he would like to be tickled under the chin and scratched behind his one remaining ear; then quite suddenly, instead of a hoarse, loud purr, Mrs. Bell would get a snarl and a smart slap, with all claws out. Soon she learnt to know from the expression on Micky's striped face and the set of his whiskers and his one ear whether he wanted to be petted or to be passed with no more than a courteous 'Good morning'.

There was the very, very old black cat, so old that her fur looked rusty in the sun, who only liked having her back stroked very gently, and a young grey one who liked to be rolled over on his back and rubbed very hard under all his four legs. There was a tortoiseshell half-

Persian who invented a private game of her own with Mrs. Bell. She would jump out from the area railings as soon as Mrs. Bell appeared

with her shopping-bag and rub round her ankles, make a tremendous fuss of her and often follow her all down the street. Then, just when Mrs. Bell was quite frightened in case the tortoiseshell followed her across the main road among all the traffic, she would stop dead and suddenly race back the way she had come, exactly like someone who has remembered an urgent appointment and hasn't time to say good-bye. And, when Mrs. Bell returned home, the tortoiseshell cat would be sitting in front of her area railings, washing herself or just staring thoughtfully into space. She *saw* Mrs. Bell, but she pretended she didn't. She simply looked straight through her as if no such person existed. Yet the very next morning, the moment Mrs. Bell appeared, there she was rubbing round her ankles and almost choking herself with flattering purrs as if she were the one human being the tortoiseshell had ever really admired.

Mrs. Bell came to know so many cats in the neighbourhood, old cats, young cats, big cats, little cats, sober cats, frisky cats, shy cats and show-off cats, that it would take a whole book to write about them all. But there was one kind of cat she never saw in the neighbourhood . . . and that was a *Siamese* cat. This was rather strange, because right opposite the house where Mrs. Bell's flat was, across the square garden, was the Siamese Embassy. Every day she saw many beautiful Siamese people with tiny feet and delicate brown hands, going in and out of the big house. But never did she see even one beautiful Siamese *cat* with delicate brown paws. The only cats she ever saw on the doorstep of the Siamese Embassy were a fat, impressive black one whose name she discovered was Winston, and a lean, spinsterish tabby with polite, but formal manners. Neither could have been more typically British.

One morning Mrs. Bell met a cat . . . or rather a half-grown kitten . . . she had never seen before. She would certainly have noticed it if she had, for it was very striking to look at. It was pure white, though a trifle grubby, and it had one blue eye and one green one. It was sitting at the corner of the garden square and the moment she came near it, it began to mew piteously. What was the matter? It certainly wasn't hurt, for, as she stopped to say a kind word to it, it ran up a tree as fast as a squirrel.

As it happened, Mrs. Bell bought fish for her lunch that day. When she reached the corner of the square, on her way home, the white cat appeared as if by magic. This time it wasn't merely mewing, it was positively yowling. And, from the way it clawed at her shopping-bag, there was no doubt what it wanted. So Mrs. Bell pulled off the head of the whiting she had bought and gave it to the white cat who gobbled it up like lightning. 'Poor thing, you must be starving,' she said. Yet, somehow, it didn't *look* as if it were starving. And the minute it had eaten the fish, up the tree it rushed again.

After that, every single morning, for five whole days, the white cat always appeared at the same corner of the square, just as Mrs. Bell passed, and always mewing pite-ously. It was obviously dreadfully, dreadfully hungry. So Mrs. Bell took to buying fish for it every morning. And

23

always, as she passed that corner of the square on her way home, the white cat would bound through the railings or leap down from a branch of the tree and devour the fish as if it were the first decent meal it had had for days. Then, having barely said 'thanks' with a short rough purr or a little butt of its white head against Mrs. Bell's legs, up the tree it would rush again.

Between these daily meetings, Mrs. Bell found herself thinking more and more about the beautiful half-grown white cat with one blue eye and one green one. Poor thing, it obviously couldn't have a home, for no cat with a home could be so dreadfully hungry as that every single morning. She took to buying it more and more fish and every scrap disappeared. It must certainly be a stray, cruelly abandoned as Victoria had been. No doubt, when it was a kitten, someone had thought it a pretty plaything, but as soon as it began to grow into a cat, they had got tired of it and turned it adrift. Mrs. Bell knew that people all too often did this cruel thing. Someone must have been very hard-hearted, she thought, to have turned such a beautiful creature out to starve. Not that the white cat *looked* starving. Probably, living wild in the garden square, it caught birds. Well, that was all right in the summer, but autumn was coming on and already the nights were chilly. When the winter came, the white kitten like all cats, however much they live outdoors, would need shelter and warmth.

By the sixth morning, Mrs. Bell's mind was made up. Since the white cat had no home and she had a home and no cat, she would adopt it. She knew it might be a slow process getting a wild, half-grown cat to trust her . . . and even to train it to home life. But, at least it would be safe and warm and no longer have to depend on chance for its breakfast. Anyhow, it had been *sent* to her, just as Victoria had been, so it was her plain duty to take it in.

Yet, though the white cat was so beautiful, she did not feel any tremendous affection for it. She was sorry for it and she admired its looks, yet somehow it left her cold. She was far fonder of gruff old Micky and the funny tortoiseshell next door who teased her by pretending not to know her. Yet the moment she had set eyes on Victoria, who had been such a very plain kitten and, from the first, had had a rather difficult character, she had known at once this was *her* cat. And Victoria had recognised Mrs. Bell at once as her mistress . . . or rather lady-in-waiting. Not only had Mrs. Bell never felt like this about the white cat, she was pretty sure he didn't feel it about her either. He seemed to take no personal interest in her except as a fish-provider.

Nevertheless, the very next morning, she set out with her shopping-bag, determined to bring back not only some extra nice fish for the white kitten, but the white kitten himself. But when she got to the usual corner of the square, there was no white kitten. Instead, there was a human being, whom she had never seen before. A plump, rosy-cheeked, friendly-looking woman was looking up into the white kitten's favourite tree and talking up into it.

'Now, come along down, Whisky, do,' said the rosy-cheeked woman. 'Come in and have your breakfast. Whisky! *Whisky!* Oh, you bad little cat, you!'

Mrs. Bell looked up into the tree herself. Peering down between the twigs and leaves was a mischievous white face with one blue eye and one green one.

'Does that beautiful little white cat belong to you?' she asked the unknown woman.

'Whisky? To be sure he does. And a naughty, artful little pussy he is too. Up to all sorts of tricks. Me and my husband have only just come to London from the country, with him and his mother Snowball, who's pure white too, like him. She settled down at once to London life but he's still a regular country tomboy, always out in the garden here, running up the trees. I'm always so frightened he'll get stolen, such a pretty kitten as he is. He gets himself dirty out here, but you should see him when Snowball's given him a good wash.'

Mrs. Bell felt her cheeks must have turned much pinker than the countrywoman's. She realised that, without knowing it, *she* had been planning to steal Whisky!

She said, with some embarrassment:

'Indeed he's a lovely young cat. I've been admiring him for days. And I'm so glad to know he has a good home. Because . . . I *almost* thought he was a stray. He's been meeting me every morning and complaining so dreadfully of hunger . . .'

The rosy-cheeked woman looked at Mrs. Bell and laughed:

'You haven't by any chance been feeding him, have you?'

'Well, I *have* been bringing him fish,' admitted Mrs. Bell.

The countrywoman laughed more than ever.

'The artfulness of him!' she said. 'He's the greediest kitten I ever did see. I'd an idea he'd been getting some extra from somewhere, for, greedy as he is, lately he's sometimes left a bit of food on his plate, instead of gobbling it all at once. I thought he'd been stealing some other cat's food as he steals his poor mother's.'

Mrs. Bell felt very foolish. Then the countrywoman called up into the tree, in an extremely angry voice:

'You wicked, lying deceiving pussy, you! Pretending to be a lone lorn hungry orphan and bringing shame on us all! Oh, you bad, bad Whisky! Taking in the kind London lady like a regular old gipsy!'

But Mrs. Bell knew she wasn't really angry, but very proud of her cunning cat. And Whisky knew it too. He jumped down from the branch of the tree and landed neatly on his mistress's shoulder. Then he rubbed his face against her rosy cheeks and purred his rough, harsh purr. When the countrywoman said good-bye and walked away with Whisky on her shoulder, the white cat looked back for a moment at Mrs. Bell. And she could almost have sworn he winked at her . . . with his *green* eye.

It is natural for someone who had gone out meaning to take a cat in to feel slightly disappointed when she finds that the cat has taken *her* in. Yet, as Mrs. Bell walked on towards the shops, mentally crossing FISH off her list, she also felt slightly relieved.

4

THE EPISODE of Whisky seemed to make it plain to Mrs.
Bell that she was not intended to have a new kitten.
By now she was getting almost used not to having a cat of
her own. She told herself she was quite happy with her
many cat friends in the neighbourhood. She also reminded
herself that a private cat needs a great deal of attention.
Surely she ought to be able to write many more pages
every day, now that she was not being constantly interrupted to open doors or clean a tray of sawdust or provide
meals or entertainment.

Certainly this *should* have been so; but, in fact, it was
not. Mrs. Bell was always making excuses to go out to the
cinema or the theatre just to get out of her big, empty
flat. And, at the end of a few weeks, she found she had
very little money left. She had spent far too much on
going out and giving herself treats. Worse still, she was so
behindhand with her new book, that there would be no
money coming in for ages.

One day, she went into a bookshop she had never been
into before, and there, fast asleep on a chair, was a beautiful *Siamese* cat. At once, all her old longing to have a
Siamese came back. She forgot all about the book she

meant to buy (which was just as well since she couldn't really afford it) and just stood admiring the cat. It had a creamy coat and a dark brown face and long dark brown stockings and she knew that if its eyes were open, they would be very blue . . . and perhaps they might squint a little.

The girl who kept the shop was quite young. She smiled when she saw Mrs. Bell looking at the Siamese.

'Are you fond of cats?' she asked.

'Yes, indeed,' said Mrs. Bell. 'Is this beautiful Siamese yours?'

'She is. Or rather, I am hers. I have to bring her to the shop every morning because she does not like being left all alone.'

'Would she mind if I stroked her?'

'Not at all. She loves to be made a fuss of.'

So Mrs. Bell stroked the Siamese cat, very carefully so as not to disturb it. Its fur felt quite different from an ordinary cat's. Though it was so smooth and fine, there was a delicious harshness about it. It was also strangely cool to the touch. Mrs. Bell felt her hand would recognise that fur as Siamese, even in the dark. The cat opened its eyes. They were grey-blue—or was it aquamarine?—in its chocolate-brown face and they were slightly crossed.

Then it started up a vibrating purr that Mrs. Bell could feel all through its body . . . a rich, *contralto* purr that made ordinary purrs seem like thin sopranos.

'Her name is Phong-Phan,' said the lucky girl who owned her. 'It means Beautiful Complexion in Siamese.'

'What a good name,' said Mrs. Bell. 'For I do think this cream and brown is the most beautiful complexion of all for a Siamese.'

'The chocolate-pointed? Yes, I agree. For though the seal-points and the blue-points are lovely too, I love the chocolate best.'

Before she realised it, Mrs. Bell was asking all sorts of questions about Siamese cats and their characters and habits. Were they as delicate as some people said? Was it true they were apt to be nervous and hysterical?

'They are the most intelligent and affectionate cats in the world,' answered the girl. 'Of course they do need to be treated with special consideration. They hate being left alone and they have very strong and sensitive feelings. But it's only if they are misunderstood that they become nervous and cross. And you must be careful to give them the right food when they are kittens and to see they don't catch chills. Then they grow into fine healthy cats who can go out in all weathers. I think they've so much charm and character—as well as beauty—that they spoil you for all other cats.'

Mrs. Bell was sure that nothing could change her

affection for plain, ordinary cats. But she did begin to feel a desperate longing to possess a Siamese.

'I'm afraid they're very expensive to buy, aren't they?'

'Well, yes . . . I was lucky to get Phong-Phan for three guineas because I have a friend who breeds Siamese. And because, though the original Siamese had squints and kinks at the end of their tails, for some reason that is no longer fashionable. Phong-Phan has a straight tail but, as she has a squint, as you see, she cannot be a show-cat.'

'Personally, I *prefer* a squint and a kinky tail,' said Mrs. Bell. 'Anyway, I'm sure no show-cat could be more beautiful than Phong-Phan.'

'Naturally, I think so too,' smiled the girl. 'But if ever you want a Siamese kitten, do buy one from a breeder. Then you're sure of getting a healthy one who has been properly fed and cared for from birth.'

'And it would cost . . . well, how much?'

'You would be lucky if you got a female for five or six guineas. A male would cost even more.'

'Oh dear,' sighed Mrs. Bell. 'I fear that is more than I could possibly afford at the moment.' She thought regretfully of all the money she had spent going out to cinemas and all the money she hadn't earned because of not staying at home and writing her book. So she said good-bye politely and regretfully to the beautiful Phong-Phan and her mistress and went home to her empty flat.

But she did get on with her writing and she thought that some day, if she was good and saved up some money, she might, in the distant future, think of buying a Siamese kitten.

5

A FEW days after her meeting with Phong-Phan, Mrs. Bell had a visit from her great friend Mrs. Grey, who lived in Rye and did not often come to London. Mrs. Grey had sympathised more deeply than anyone over the death of Victoria. And, like Mrs. Black and Mrs. White, she had urged Mrs. Bell to adopt a new kitten.

'Now, my dear,' said Mrs. Grey, 'the time really has come to consider the question seriously. You have mourned long enough for dear Victoria. Besides, I can see in your eyes that you are no longer so firm in your resolution *never* to have another.'

Mrs. Bell had to admit this was so. She told Mrs. Grey the story of the deceitful Whisky. But she did *not* mention Phong-Phan and her talk with the girl in the bookshop.

There were two reasons for this. One was that she knew Mrs. Grey wanted to *give* her a kitten. And, if she had realised Mrs. Bell secretly longed for a Siamese, she would have bought her one, for she was very generous. But Mrs. Grey was not at all rich and Mrs. Bell would have hated her to give her something she could not afford. The

34

other reason was a rather queer one . . . and it had been worrying her ever since she had begun to think of saving up to buy a Siamese. It was this. Every year, hundreds of charming ordinary kittens are born who desperately need good homes and don't always get them. But a precious, luxury Siamese kitten is practically sure of a good home because people are proud to possess these rare cats and willing to pay a lot of money for them. So a person who truly loved cats would be showing more kindness by taking in an ordinary kitten whom no one but a genuine cat-lover would cherish and appreciate.

Mrs. Grey said:

'I have been thinking for weeks what kind of kitten might suit you. As you know, the cats of Rye, though simple tabbies, blacks, marmalades, tortoiseshell and so on, are particularly large and handsome. They are famous throughout Sussex and many foreign visitors exclaim over their exceptional size and splendid fur.'

'That is so, indeed,' agreed Mrs. Bell. 'Your own two fine black cats, Torky and Boudy, both Rye born and bred, are excellent examples.'

'Boudy has no kittens in prospect at the moment. And in any case, her kittens are nearly always black or black-and-white. I am sure you would greatly prefer your future kitten to be of an entirely different colour to Victoria. Have you anything in mind?'

Mrs. Bell thought for a moment. Then, dismissing all fancies of cream cats with chocolate stockings, she said:

'If ever I *did* have another kitten . . . I believe I could

fancy a marmalade one, like Orlando. As you know, I
have the honour to know that famous cat and it has given
me a particular affection for cats of his colour. I believe
the official name is Red Tabby but marmalade describes
it so perfectly. And I have never possessed a true, all-
over marmalade. Fury had ginger ears and a ginger tail
and a ginger saddle on his back but he was three-quarters
white.'

'Splendid,' said Mrs. Grey. 'We will consider the
matter settled. The minute I get back to Rye I will start
making inquiries. I do not know of any marmalade
kittens about at the moment but I will find out if there are
any prospective mothers who might be likely to produce
them. It may be many weeks before I can find you one
but find you one I will. Marmalades are usually male,
which would make your new cat even more different
from Victoria.'

When Mrs. Grey had gone, Mrs. Bell felt positively
cheerful. Really it would be very nice indeed . . . perhaps
before Christmas . . . to have a marmalade kitten frisking
about her big empty flat. It was the beginning of October
now and cold enough at night to light a fire. And, as the
days grew shorter and darker, how pleasant it would be to
see a cat curled up on her hearthrug again. Though she
was beginning to miss Victoria less, she knew she would
begin to miss her dreadfully again when winter came.
Besides there *was* something exciting about the thought
of a kitten . . . a frisky, gay kitten getting up to every kind
of mischief and inventing all sorts of wild games. Victoria

had lived to such a great age that it was almost impossible to remember she had ever been a kitten and just as playful as any other . . . though, to be honest, less purry and cuddly than most.

So Mrs. Bell found herself wondering whether the marmalade kitten which, of course, would have blue eyes at first, would grow up to have green eyes or amber ones. And she would stop writing her book to put down what seemed possible names for marmalade cats and to write such things as:

MEM.

Ping-pong ball.

Cork on string.

Feather on elastic?

New tray (pref. enamel).

Sawdust (still have sack in attic).

Basket? (will probably prefer bed).

Log for claw-sharpening (almost certainly won't use).

Only a few days after Mrs. Grey had returned to Rye, Mrs. Bell received a letter from her. It said:

'I have hopeful news for you but don't get too excited yet because we shall not know for *at least* another fortnight. The other day I followed a splendid tortoiseshell cat, who was soon going to have kittens, back to her home. On making inquiries of her owner, I find this cat, whose name is Mamma, because she is such an admirable mother, bears the most excellent character, being a retired ship's cat. Moreover, as her husband is black and not only a fine specimen, but highly respected throughout Rye, the children of such parents should be healthy, handsome and of good disposition. As you know, there is often at least one marmalade in the litter of a tortoiseshell mother and a black father, and Mamma has frequently produced them. Her mistress has promised that if there is a marmalade male in this next lot . . . due about October 11th . . . it shall be kept for you. I will let you know the moment the kittens are born and I *do* hope there will be a marmalade for you.'

Mrs. Bell hoped so too, and she began to cross off the days on her calendar to October 11th. And every morning when she went out shopping she spoke to her various cat friends, gruff old Micky and naughty young Whisky (whom she had quite forgiven) and all the others, with new confidence and even a touch of authority because she might soon be going to have a cat of her own again. And to the teasing tortoiseshell who liked to pretend she didn't know her, she said: ' My dear, a joke's a joke, but you can carry it too far as I am sure Mamma, the tortoiseshell cat of Rye, formerly of the Royal Merchant Navy, would agree.

'Perhaps one of these mornings, I shall pretend *I* don't know *you*!'

6

MRS. BELL had crossed only three days off her calendar when the most *extraordinary* thing happened. As she was sitting writing at her desk, the telephone bell rang. She picked up the receiver and a man's voice, which she did not recognise at first, because she had not heard it for a long time, said:

'Is that Mrs. Bell?'

'Yes, speaking.'

She recognised the voice now; it belonged to her old friend Colonel Brown. Colonel Brown was a great lover of animals. He was a great expert on horses but he also knew a great deal about cats and dogs and had many friends who bred them.

'I have some news that might interest you,' said Colonel Brown. 'I was so sorry to hear from Mrs. White that you had lost Victoria. If you have not yet got another cat, I wonder if you would care to have a very charming Siamese kitten.'

Mrs. Bell could hardly believe her ears. Her mind went into a kind of foggy whirl. She said faintly:

'A . . . *Siamese* . . . kitten . . .?'

'Yes. Chocolate-pointed. I know the breeder very well.

Kitten's a female between three and four months old . . .
splendid pedigree . . . absolutely healthy . . . very intelligent . . . remarkably friendly . . . Tempted to have her
myself, but I've one cat and two dogs as it is . . .'

Mrs. Bell came to her senses a little.

'How kind of you to think of me,' she said. 'But I am
afraid I couldn't afford a pedigree Siamese. And, actually,
I've already got a kitten in prospect.'

Her voice must have gone faint with surprise and emo-
tion for Colonel Brown did not seem to hear her last
words. For he broke in on them with a chuckle.

'Aha, that's the beauty of it, you won't *have* to afford it!
Because this kitten is free, gratis and for nothing. All my
friend who bred her wants is a *really* good home for her.
And I couldn't think of any home I could more strongly
recommend than yours, now that I understand it is
vacant.'

Mrs. Bell felt most violently tempted. She just couldn't
help asking:

'But why should anyone want to *give* away such a valu-
able kitten when they could get a lot of money for it?'

'I thought you'd ask that. For two reasons. One, my
friend breeds cats for shows and this kitten, though very
well bred, is a throwback to the original Siamese type . . .
squint and kinky tail . . . and for some reason, judges don't
like 'em any more. Two, my friend gave the kitten as a
present to a little boy, but his father unexpectedly got a
job abroad and took the whole family with him but it
wasn't possible to take the kitten. So Minka . . . that's her

name . . . has gone back to her original home. My friends love her, but they've already three Siamese cats and more kittens coming along so they just *can't* keep her as a pet. They hate parting with her and they'll only do it to someone who will really love and appreciate her. So my very *first* suggestion was you.'

Mrs. Bell could not help being flattered. More than this, the temptation had become almost *unbearable*. A chocolate-pointed Siamese kitten with a squint and a kinky tail wanting a good home and hers for the asking! But she just *had* to be honest. So she told Colonel Brown all about Mrs. Grey and how much trouble she had taken and how, in a week or two, there *might* be a marmalade kitten being specially kept for her.

Colonel Brown said:

'Come, come, kitten isn't even born yet. There's many a slip 'twixt the cup and the lip. Very likely this tortoiseshell won't produce a marmalade this time. Think what a wonderful chance you'll have missed. You don't often find a first-class Siamese going begging.'

'No, indeed,' said poor Mrs. Bell. She was almost in tears from being placed in such a terrible dilemma. 'Oh dear, it's so frightfully tempting . . . I've always *longed* for a Siamese . . . But then . . . if there should be a marmalade . . . and my friend has been so kind . . . it's almost a question of *honour*.'

Being a soldier, Colonel Brown quite saw her point. He said understandingly:

'I see that. Still, you don't have to make up your mind

at once. In any case, you'd have to look at the Siamese first. Who knows, you mightn't take to each other. Even if you do, you don't have to commit yourself.'

'No, I needn't, need I?' said Mrs. Bell more cheerfully.

'Splendid. I'll give you the Greens' address.' So she carefully wrote down the address and Colonel Brown said:

'Good-bye . . . and best of luck to your kitten-hunting

 . . . whatever breed you finally bring home.' And just before he rang off, he added slyly: 'The more the merrier.'

That very afternoon, Mrs. Bell set off to that address. Even if she couldn't have the Siamese herself, there was no harm in looking at her. Besides she might be able to suggest some other good home for Minka. However, she was so busy telling herself she couldn't possibly have the kitten . . . anyhow until she was sure Mamma had not produced a marmalade one . . . that she arrived at the house without even thinking of other possible homes for the Siamese.

Mrs. Green was not at home, but her twin daughters were. In front of a fire sat a beautiful grown-up chocolate-pointed Siamese cat and beside her was a fine kitten about three months old. But this kitten had a long, straight tail and no squint so Mrs. Bell knew it could not be Minka. From the distance came the resonant, metallic miaowing of other Siamese cats.

The twin called Mary said:

'The grown-up cat is Minka's mother, Coco. She is such a sweet, affectionate cat . . . we think Minka takes after her. The kitten is Minka's brother, Macaroon. He's not as bright as Minka. But he's such a perfect specimen that we're sure he'll be a champion.'

When Mrs. Bell had admired and stroked the two beautiful cats, the twin called Jane, whom Mrs. Bell couldn't tell from her sister (they were so much alike and each as pretty as the other), said:

'I see you love cats. Oh, I *do* hope you will have Minka. She's much the cleverest and most amusing of Coco's last three kittens so we do want her to go where she'll be appreciated.'

Mrs. Bell now had to explain her difficult situation and the twins were very sympathetic. Jane said:

'Well, you'll know in a fortnight whether Mamma has a marmalade kitten or not. If she doesn't, we *might* still have Minka. Unfortunately, someone else is interested. But we'd far rather *you* had her.'

Mary said: 'But first Mrs. Bell must see if she likes her.'

She went out of the room and came back with a kitten in her arms. It had a very small, three-cornered brown face with enormous blue eyes that squinted slightly. And the brown tail that hung down below Mary's arm had a funny little crook at the very end.

Mrs. Bell looked into the kitten's eyes and they looked back into hers. In spite of the squint, they obviously saw very clearly indeed. Then, suddenly, the kitten sprang out of Mary's arms straight into Mrs. Bell's lap, purring loudly. She was so light that Mrs. Bell could hardly feel her weight on her knee but her purr was so penetrating that it seemed to go all through Mrs. Bell as if she were purring herself.

'Oh, you darling,' said Mrs. Bell, stroking the cream-coloured coat softly with one finger. As she did so, she noticed, as she had with Phong-Phan, the coolness and the firm texture of Siamese fur. With every stroke, the kitten's purr grew stronger and stronger and Mrs. Bell's honourable resolution weaker and weaker.

'There, you see,' exclaimed the twins together. 'Minka's obviously made up *her* mind.'

'Oh dear,' said poor Mrs. Bell, 'I don't know how to *resist* this kitten.' For the moment Minka had sprung on her lap, something like a tiny electric shock had gone through her and told her: 'This is *your* cat and you both know it.'

'Then *don't* resist her,' said Jane with a smile.

And Mary said:

'It's no good your trying. Minka has a very determined character.'

'Yes, indeed,' said Jane. 'And, friendly as she is to all human beings, we have never seen her take such a violent fancy to one at first sight.'

'I am deeply flattered,' said Mrs. Bell, 'and it's love at

44

first sight with me too. Oh dear, I don't know how to bear the suspense of the next two weeks. To think, through waiting for a kitten who may never exist, I may lose the real live Minka.'

Mary said hopefully:

'Why not have her . . . and, if there's a marmalade kitten . . . have him too?'

But Jane shook her head.

'Mary, Mrs. Bell must know the truth. Minka has one serious fault—her jealousy of other cats. She behaves quite well to her mother but she bullies and snubs poor Macaroon quite shockingly when Coco's back is turned. As to her sister Sapphire, she treated her so unkindly that we were thankful that Sapphire had gone to her new home before Minka returned to us.'

Minka evidently knew she was being talked about. Her pointed brown ears twitched and she stopped purring. She twisted her head round and squinted up into Mrs. Bell's face with an expression that said very clearly:

'I'm much nicer than Macaroon, aren't I? And twenty times more intelligent!'

Then she squinted down at Macaroon and gave a contemptuous yawn. Macaroon looked rather offended. Then he got up, walked deliberately over to Mrs. Bell and politely sniffed her ankles. He was a most beautiful Siamese kitten, with a perfectly shaped face and a long tapering tail. But Mrs. Bell dared not even stroke the top of his dark brown head for Minka had at once begun to snarl

45

under her breath. One did not have to know Siamese language to guess the sort of thing she was saying.

'Yah, rat's tail . . . Ffff . . . Mummy's precious *straight-eyed* boy . . . Keep off my human being, will you?'

And then she snuggled up close to Mrs. Bell and began to purr so violently that she nearly choked herself, to show that she had no intention of being rude to *her*.

'Oh dear,' said poor Mrs. Bell. 'I'm *terribly* attracted to Minka and she seems to like me too. But I see that, like my old cat Victoria, she just wouldn't tolerate a rival. It would have to be Minka and no one *but* Minka in my home. So alas, there's nothing I can do but wait for the news from Rye.'

She stood up to say good-bye, for every moment was making it harder for her to keep her resolution and not take Minka home with her there and then. When she tried, very gently, to put Minka down, the Siamese kitten clung to her, clambered up on her shoulder, knocked her hat crooked and purred right into her ear. Mrs. Bell said, as Jane removed Minka with difficulty:

'Oh, Minka . . . I *know* . . . But I *must* wait . . . Perhaps it will all come right in the end.'

Jane laughed and said:

'Minka will see that it does. Anyway, we'll keep her for you as long as we possibly can.'

And Mary whispered:

'If you *do* make up your mind sooner, you have only to ring us up. We'll have her ready for you at an hour's notice.'

46

When Mrs. Bell got back to her flat, she could think of
nothing but that cream kitten with the tiny dark face and
the big squinting blue eyes and the absurd kink at the end
of her tail. She did not even dare go into the room where
the telephone was. She went to bed early but she did not
sleep much—her mind was in such a whirl. And when
she did sleep, she kept dreaming of Minka so vividly that
it was as if she were really there. But every now and then
in her dreams, she kept hearing a small plaintive mew. It
seemed to be saying, 'Mrs. Be-e-ell, what about me-e-e?'
And she knew that it came from an invisible marmalade
kitten.

7

THE NEXT morning Mrs. Bell was having such a fierce argument with herself that she hardly touched her breakfast. Just as she had finished the argument by saying to herself very severely: 'It would be wrong even to *think* of it,' she suddenly pushed away her cup of tea and ran upstairs. The next minute she was staring at the telephone on her desk. And the next, she had picked up the receiver and was dialling the Greens' number.

When she heard a voice at the other end, she said, all in one breath:

'Mrs. Bell speaking and I know I oughtn't to but I just can't bear to risk losing her so please may I fetch her at eleven o'clock and I'll bring my own basket.'

The voice of a twin (she'd no idea which) said:

'Splendid! We *knew* Minka would get her way!'

Without waiting to clear away her breakfast or even put on her hat, Mrs. Bell rushed straight out to the shops. There was so much to be done, for she had nothing ready for the reception of a New Kitten. She was in such a hurry, that she only said a very brief 'Good morning' to the various cats of her acquaintance she met on the way, though for once they *all* seemed to be in the mood for a long chat.

She bought some nice fresh fish and a bottle of milk and a ping-pong ball and a lovely new white enamel tray with high sides. Then she went quickly home and nearly ran up all the six flights of stairs. She put the fish to boil in the kitchen and then she went up to the attic at the very top of the house. From there she fetched a bag of sawdust and the big wicker cat-basket with a lid to it. As she brought them downstairs, she heard the front door open and knew that Mrs. Silver had arrived.

'Dear me,' said Mrs. Silver. 'Fish cooking at this time of the morning! Why, it's like old times ... And, gracious, you've actually got the cat-basket ... *Could* it mean ... ?'

'Yes, Mrs. Silver, it could!' said Mrs. Bell excitedly. 'In an hour or two ... I shall be bringing home ... a ... Siamese ... kitten ... For *good* ...'

Mrs. Silver, who loved cats, became as excited as Mrs. Bell. 'A kitten about the place again,' she cried. 'How wonderful! But this is so sudden . . . And you said Siamese!'

'I'll tell you all later on,' panted Mrs. Bell. 'But now there is no time to be lost. I'm fetching her at eleven.'

'Then there certainly isn't,' said Mrs. Silver. 'Leave the cooking to me. I'll finish off the fish, take the bones out and chop it up small. You get on with the basket and the rest.'

So Mrs. Bell scrubbed the cat-basket which was dusty from not having been used for many years and put lots of clean newspaper in it with a nice soft piece of old blanket folded on top. And she put sawdust in the beautiful new white tray and put the tray in a place that was both secluded, yet easy for a kitten to reach. Cats are clean by nature and it is nearly always their owner's fault if they make messes in the wrong places. They are modest and fastidious and like their trays kept nice and fresh and in not too public a place.

Having arranged for this important side of Minka's needs, Mrs. Bell scrubbed out the little sleeping-basket that Victoria had outgrown many years ago, put another bit of clean blanket in it and set it by her desk, in front of the fire. The twins had told her that Siamese, having originally come from a hot climate, needed warmth. And she knew from Phong-Phan's mistress that they liked to be constantly with their human beings. Of course *any* kitten, suddenly removed from its family, needs to be cherished when it comes to its new home and not left all on its own. But Siamese need it even when they are full-grown.

All was ready just in time. Just as eleven o'clock was striking, Mrs. Bell arrived at the Greens' house. The twins had been busy too. They had written out a list of meals called MINKA'S MENU and made lovely drawings of Minka eating them. There were to be four meals at first—all little ones—because she was only three and a half months old and one was to be 'tea' of Farex and milk. They warned Mrs. Bell she must only give Minka just so many ounces of fish or rabbit at each meal, however much she yowled for more. At six months, she was to have 'tea' but no 'lunch' and at a year, just two good meals, one fish and one meat, morning and evening.

'All Siamese are greedy,' said Jane. 'And I am afraid Minka is specially so. But don't give in to her, for her own sake, or you'll make her ill. The reason lots of people think Siamese are delicate is that they don't feed them right when they are young. Stick to MINKA'S MENU and she'll grow into a fine, healthy cat.'

'And don't forget,' chimed in Mary, 'always to have a bowl of fresh water where she can get at it, just as if she were a dog. All Siamese need to drink a lot of water.'

'I know that even ordinary cats should have water as well as milk,' said Mrs. Bell. 'Because milk is really a food, not a drink. But I will be most careful to do so.'

Mrs. Bell was beginning to feel as nervous as a mother bringing home her first baby from the hospital. She had brought up many kittens, but taking on one's first Siamese seemed a great responsibility. And when the twins gave her a paper on which Minka's pedigree was set out (and from which she discovered that her full name was Minka-Pi and that her registered number was 69598 of Siamese Breed 24 B . . . chocolate-pointed) she felt more responsible than ever. Suppose she did something wrong? Suppose this highly-bred kitten did not thrive as she should? It would serve her right for having snatched at this young Princess instead of waiting to see whether two sturdy yeoman cats had produced a sturdy yeoman kitten with no champions in his ancestry and not even belonging to any breed recognised by the Cat Fancy.

But when Jane went out of the room and came back with Minka in her arms (she hadn't brought her in at first because she knew Minka would have distracted Mrs. Bell from her lesson on How to Bring up a Siamese), all her fears went. As soon as she saw that small dark face and those huge squinting aquamarine eyes and heard that outsize purr, Mrs. Bell didn't worry any more about her being an Eastern Princess. She was her very own Minka and she couldn't wait to get her home.

Minka herself seemed to be in quite as much of a hurry. After one sniff at the open cat-basket, she climbed into it and sat down without any fuss. The twins stroked her and kissed her good-bye, and very carefully Mrs. Bell strapped down the lid and carried the basket away. It hardly weighed any more with Minka in it than when it was empty.

But once out in the street, a most dreadful yowling and scrabbling started inside the basket. It was obvious Minka did not at all like being shut up. And all the way home in the bus, the yowling and scrabbling went on and people kept saying:

'Oo, poor little kitty!' and 'What a shame!' and 'Open the lid and let's have a dekko, ducks!'

Mrs. Bell held the basket as steady as she could on her knee. She did not dare open the lid for fear Minka should escape. She kept looking through the air-holes and sometimes she could see one indignant squinting blue eye or a pointed brown ear. Once, a delicate brown paw, hardly bigger than a thimble, came out through the hole. Mrs. Bell stroked it soothingly but it disappeared back through the hole as quick as a snake.

After what seemed hours, Mrs. Bell at last found herself carrying the precious basket up her own six flights of stairs. She could feel Minka jumping about inside it and the Siamese voice sounded decidedly impatient. When she reached her front door, she did not wait to find her latchkey but rang the bell. Mrs. Silver came running down to open the door.

'I knew you'd got her,' she exclaimed. 'I heard her voice all up the stairs. You said a *kitten* . . . But she *sounds* grown-up.'

'It's the Siamese voice,' said Mrs. Bell. 'Come into my study where it's warmest and you shall see for yourself what size she is.'

In front of the fire, they both knelt beside the basket and lifted the lid. For one moment, Minka crouched down in it looking very small and frightened. Then with one spring, she bounded up on to Mrs. Bell's shoulder and clung there with all twenty tiny sharp claws, rubbing her dark face against Mrs. Bell's cheek and purring almost as loud as she had been yowling.

'Oh, you little beauty!' said Mrs. Silver. 'Why, her eyes are almost the colour of bluebells . . . the pale ones, not the dark. And I like her funny little squint . . . it gives her face such character.'

'Yes, doesn't it?' said Mrs. Bell proudly. 'And look at the kink at the end of her tail. I like that too even though it means she's an old-fashioned Siamese and hasn't got the New Look they expect in show-cats.'

'Just hark at that purr! Poor Victoria was never one for purring, was she? But, for all her size, I'm sure she couldn't have purred so loud as that. Why, this little thing is such a mite, you wouldn't think she had the strength to make all that noise. How old is she? Six weeks?'

'No, more than twice that. She'll be a small cat, even when she's grown up.'

'And doesn't she love you already? I don't suppose she'll let me stroke her. They say they only care for one person.'

'Try and see. I think you'll find she's very friendly.'

So Mrs. Silver stroked and Minka obviously liked it very much.

'Hasn't she got delicate little whiskers? As fine as cobwebs. Everything about her is so beautifully finished off . . . Like a little miniature cat, more than a kitten.'

Minka obviously enjoyed all this admiration. Then suddenly she got bored with it. She jumped down on to the carpet and stalked all over the room, with her kinky tail held high, sniffing into every corner and looking under the bookshelves and Mrs. Bell's desk. Then she stalked back to the fire, sat down in front of it, carefully licked one tiny brown paw and began calmly to wash her face.

'Did you ever?' said Mrs. Silver. 'Look how she's settled down. Why, she looks almost grown-up, sitting there as if she'd lived here for years, as staid as you please.'

But the next moment, Minka stopped being staid and grown-up. She leapt across the room, quick as a little hare, and ran half-way up a curtain. She was so light that the curtain hardly sagged but she couldn't think how to get down again so she clung there like a burr and yowled for help. But no sooner had Mrs. Bell rescued her than she bounded out of her arms and on to the back of a chair. From there she leapt on to another chair and up on the mantelpiece and from one thing to another till Mrs. Bell and Mrs. Silver got quite giddy watching her.

'She's going to be a regular handful,' said Mrs. Bell. 'But see how daintily she jumps . . . she hasn't upset a thing.'

Quite suddenly Minka stopped her wild game and sat down primly again, with her kinky tail wrapped round her front paws. Then a thoughtful expression appeared on her face. She began to creep slowly across the carpet, making for a dark corner. Mrs. Bell knew the signs.

'Quick,' she called to Mrs. Silver, 'open the door. She wants her tray.'

With a deft pounce, she picked up Minka and carried

55

her out to her tray, just in time. Minka knew at once what the clean sawdust was for and carefully rearranged it when she had finished. '*Good* Minka,' said Mrs. Bell and stroked her. She knew how important it was for a kitten to be shown at once where its official lavatory was before it had time to make choice of an unofficial one for itself. As they usually go back to the *first* place, it is much more satisfactory for all parties if the first place happens to be the *right* one.

Neither Mrs. Bell nor Mrs. Silver did much work for what was left of the morning. They were too busy playing with Minka and admiring her and keeping her from getting shut into cupboards for she was as inquisitive as a monkey and as all-over-the-place as quicksilver. She took a great fancy to Mrs. Silver and offered to help with the washing-up. But she overbalanced on the edge of the sink and plunged one hind leg and her kinky tail in the soapy water. You never saw anything so thin and bedraggled as Minka's chocolate-brown stocking and tail looked when they were wet. But she was soon dried with the kitchen towel and she began to purr round Mrs. Silver's ankles and say she thought some fish would be just the thing to restore her completely.

Mrs. Bell said she could have some as it was now her lunch-time. Minka ate it eagerly and said: 'More, please!' very imperiously. But Mrs. Bell remembered MINKA'S MENU and was firm. Minka gave a rather cross miaow that said: 'Goodness, you're as bad as they were at home!' but she let herself be picked up and carried to the basket in front of Mrs. Bell's study fire. In a moment she yawned, then the brown lids came down like shutters over the blue eyes and, when Mrs. Silver came up to say good-bye, the cream-coloured kitten was rolled up in a neat ball, fast asleep.

8

MINKA SLEPT for two whole hours. Though Mrs. Bell *tried* to do some writing, she kept looking down at what lay in the basket at her feet and saying to herself: 'She really and truly belongs to me. I simply can't believe it.'

Have you ever been given a wonderful present from a Christmas tree—something you've always longed for? When you've unwrapped it in front of other people and admired it and said 'Thank you', you're still a little bit dazed. It isn't till you get it all by yourself and handle it and examine it close to that you really take in the fact that it is your very own.

That was exactly how Mrs. Bell felt as she kept glancing down at Minka. She began to long for her to wake up. Curled up like that with her eyes tight shut and her face hidden in her paws, Mrs. Bell couldn't see nearly enough of her. But she knew it would be unkind to wake her before she had had her sleep out. All kittens need plenty of sleep and Minka needed it specially today after all the excitement of coming to a new home.

At last Mrs. Bell's patience was rewarded. Minka

yawned, stretched, uncurled herself and stood up in her basket, blinking her blue eyes and looking round her with a slightly dazed expression. So then Mrs. Bell lifted her on to her lap and, as she stroked her and talked to her,  she was able to notice all the things that made her chocolate-pointed Siamese different from any kitten she had had before.

Instead of a pink nose, she had a brown one to match her brown ears and the fur mask through which her blue eyes gleamed like aquamarines set in brown velvet. *Were* they aquamarine or pale sapphire or, as Mrs. Silver said, bluebell? Their colour kept shimmering and changing round the great black pupils with their slight inward cast. The brown mask shaded off into stripes between her ears, leaving two cream patches above her eyebrows that matched the rest of her smooth, cream-coloured fur. Mrs. Bell stroked her long brown socks and felt the absurd kink at the end of her short brown tail. It felt just as if there were a piece of bent wire inside the fur. The lining of her ears and her mouth was not the pink of ordinary cats, but a delicate mauve. Her whiskers and eyebrows were cream-colour, so fine you could hardly see them. But what fascinated Mrs. Bell almost most of all were her paws. They were oval instead of round, and so small and beautifully shaped that they seemed to be designed only for dancing or playing with elegant trifles. However, Mrs.

Bell soon discovered they were very muscular indeed and the tiny brown claws that matched them were as strong as steel and as sharp as needles.

By the end of that first day, Mrs. Bell had begun to know quite a lot about Minka. Never before had she had such a loving cat. You only had to touch her and she began to throb all over with purring as if you had pressed a switch and started up a dynamo. But she saw too that Minka had a passionate and determined character. As one of her passions was curiosity, Mrs. Bell had to keep opening and shutting doors for her to show her every corner of the flat. And, as she insisted on exploring every cupboard and every basin and scrambling on top of everything and creeping under everything, and squeezing herself behind beds and trying to jump through the banisters, Mrs. Bell had to keep her eyes skinned not to lose her or let her hurt herself.

She was a wonderfully intelligent kitten. In a few hours she had learnt that the kitchen, where food was served, was downstairs. And though she was so small that the stairs were difficult to manage, she would get down several on her own before asking Mrs. Bell for help. After each meal she said 'Thank you' very nicely, rubbing against her mistress's ankles. This was, also, of course, a try-on for a second helping. But when she saw it was not coming, she gave one surprised look, climbed up Mrs. Bell and purred to show there was no ill feeling. She quickly learnt to mew when she wanted her tray, and if Mrs.

Bell did not get her there in time, she would give her a reproachful look that said: 'How *slow* you human beings are.' And, even if it was too late, she would scrabble most industriously in the tray to show that she was an extremely well-brought-up kitten and knew what trays were for.

At bedtime, Mrs. Bell took Minka's basket into her bedroom and put it beside her own bed. She propped the door open so that she could quickly rush Minka out to her tray if she wanted it. She put Minka in the basket but Minka was in no mood for sleep. All the time Mrs. Bell was undressing she was playing mad games. She worried her stockings and nibbled at her bare toes. She jumped up on the basin and knocked the toothbrush out of her hand when she was cleaning her teeth. She clawed hold of the end of her dressing-gown belt and swung on it like a bell-rope. Even when Mrs. Bell got into bed and turned the light out, she could still hear Minka scampering wildly about the room and making soft thuds, hardly louder than a ball of wool, when she leapt down from a chair. Then there was silence, followed by a slight rustle. Had Minka settled at last into her basket? No, there was something moving very softly over Mrs. Bell's eiderdown. She lay very quiet and the something . . . it didn't seem to have any weight but she could hear the faint scratch of claws on silk . . . crept nearer and nearer. And at last she could feel smooth cool fur against her left shoulder and butterfly whiskers tickling her cheek.

There was a little padding and settling, then, right in her ear, sounded a loud contented purr. Minka had decided for herself the only proper place for a Siamese kitten to sleep.

9

A FORTNIGHT went by in no time at all. Every day Minka became more playful, more loving and more intelligent. She also became more artful and more insistent on getting her own way. In fact, she was every bit as much of a tyrant as Victoria had been but she got her own way by coaxing not by bullying and she was so charming to look at and affectionate that all Mrs. Bell's friends, even Mrs. Black, fell in love with her at sight. She was gay and friendly with all human beings but she loved Mrs. Bell best and, after her, Mrs. Silver. She was also very fond of Alice, the girl who had two rooms in Mrs. Bell's flat, and often visited her in the evenings when she came home from work. But she never slept anywhere but on Mrs. Bell's left shoulder where she snuggled down every night with a contented little sigh. Mrs. Bell had never heard a cat sigh before. Nor had she ever seen a cat wrinkle its forehead in a frown just like a human being when it was puzzled or cross. But then, she had never before had a Siamese.

Among Minka's many admirers was a young married couple who lived in the flat below. Mr. and Mrs. McGregor admired her so much that they decided that, as soon as they could find a nice one, they would have a Siamese kitten themselves.

And then, just when everyone was so busy admiring Minka and saying how enchanting she was, that there almost seemed to be no other cats in the world except Siamese, Mrs. Bell had a letter from her friend Mrs. Grey in Rye. It said:

'I have splendid news for you. Mamma had her kittens yesterday and in the litter there is one marmalade short-haired male . . . obviously *just* what you want. I've definitely booked him for you. He'll be ready to leave his mother in six weeks' time, so can you come down to Rye and fetch him then . . . say about November 30th? It's a pity he's so far from London for you must be dying to see him, but I'll report his progress and six weeks will soon pass . . . How lovely to think it won't be long till you're no longer lonely and catless!'

Mrs. Bell felt terribly guilty. For she simply hadn't had courage to tell Mrs. Grey about Minka. She kept putting it off in the hopes that, after all, Mamma would not have a marmalade among her kittens. Then she could have said . . . though it would not have been *quite* true . . . that, as she had been offered a Siamese, she would accept it.

There was nothing for it but to write a full confession, which she did. Yet, how could she refuse the marmalade kitten which her friend had taken so much trouble to find for her? After all, there *was* plenty of room for two in her flat. And how charming they would look playing together, the all-golden kitten and the pale creamy one with the dark shadows on her fur. They would be like the sun and the moon. She glanced at Minka who was sitting on her desk, trying to knock her pen out of her hand with a delicate brown paw. Oh dear, the moon-kitten was frowning. She almost certainly didn't want a rival about. She was now four months old; by the time the other kitten arrived, she would be almost half-grown. For all her fairylike looks, she was very tough. She could make life very unpleasant indeed for a baby of six weeks if she took a dislike to him before he'd grown strong enough to stand up to her.

Mrs. Bell thought hard for a long time before she finished her letter. It was almost as if Minka read her thoughts. She kept trying to sit on the writing-paper and rubbing against Mrs. Bell's cheek and purring rather aggressively as if to say:

'Do stop all this nonsense and come and play with me. I am Minka, the moon-kitten, the most intelligent cat in the world. I am also a Princess and require homage and exclusive attention.'

Mrs. Bell stroked her strongly and roughly as she had discovered her Siamese liked to be stroked. Minka closed her eyes and licked Mrs. Bell's hand appreciatively.

'Minka,' said Mrs. Bell, stroking hard, 'I couldn't love

you more dearly. But I *can't* spend all my time fussing over you and neither can Mrs. Silver. We both have work to do. Don't you think it would be nice to have another kitten to play with so that you weren't so dependent on human beings?'

Minka merely butted her head impatiently against Mrs. Bell's hand as if to say:

'Don't talk . . . You're not concentrating on your stroking. *Harder*, please.'

'That's enough, Minka,' said Mrs. Bell quite severely. 'I *must* finish my letter.'

She put her gently down on the floor. Minka was offended, turned her back and began to lash her kinky tail.

'She really is getting a tiny bit spoilt,' thought Mrs. Bell. But there was no doubt that Minka's feelings were highly sensitive and that she was passionately attached to her mistress. Suppose she were so jealous of the marmalade kitten that she not only made his life a misery but became miserable herself?

All the same, Mrs. Bell decided she would at least try the experiment. So she finished her letter to Mrs. Grey and said she would come to Rye on November 30th and collect the kitten.

It was lucky Mrs. Grey was so understanding about cats *and* human beings. She wrote back by return saying *she* wouldn't have been able to resist the offer of a Siamese either (which made Mrs. Bell feel very much better) and ending up, 'I'm so glad you're going to try having both.

Minka sounds adorable. The marmalade is sweet, though of course his eyes aren't even open yet. If Minka *doesn't* take to him (I know *you* will when you see him), *of course* she has first rights. If, after a few weeks, the situation is impossible, don't worry. I will find Kitten 2 another good home. Mamma's progeny are always in demand here. But I DO hope they get on famously and you keep both!'

This being happily settled, Mrs. Bell was much relieved. For the next fortnight, Minka behaved beautifully. She let Mrs. Bell and Mrs. Silver get on with their work quite a lot and seemed to be trying hard to amuse herself on her own. And sometimes when Mrs. Bell glanced up and saw Minka playing with a ping-pong ball and then having to rush and hit it back again herself, she thought: 'I'm sure she'll find it much more fun when there's another kitten to play ping-pong with.'

One morning there was a knock at Mrs. Bell's door. It was young Mrs. McGregor from the flat downstairs. She had a cat-basket under her arm.

'I couldn't resist bringing them to see you,' she said. 'You see it's really because of Minka that we bought them. She should be flattered, because they're chocolate-points too.'

She opened the basket and inside were two enchanting Siamese kittens, a little younger than Minka. They were very like her, except that they had straight tails and did not squint.

'Oh, what darlings,' said Mrs. Bell. 'And *two*!'

'They're brother and sister,' explained Mrs. McGregor. 'We only meant to have *one*. But they seemed so fond of each other, we hadn't the heart to separate them. They will be wonderful company for each other. May I bring them in and introduce them to Minka? Perhaps she'll like to come and play with them too.'

Minka was nowhere to be found. Then she was discovered in a box under the kitchen sink which was a place she retired to when she was sulky.

Mrs. Bell picked her up and stroked her saying:

'Here's a surprise for you, Minka. Come and be introduced.'

Mrs. McGregor stroked her too, but Minka did not purr for her as usual. She was looking at the basket with a very suspicious expression.

'I'd better hold her,' said Mrs. Bell.

The basket was opened and the kittens lifted out. They gave friendly little mews when they saw another Siamese. Not so Minka. She struggled in Mrs. Bell's arms and began to spit and swear. The next moment she leapt to the ground and began to stalk towards the kittens with her back humped and her fur on end and her tail fluffed out to three times its size like a bottle-brush. She was giving

alarming hoarse growls that Mrs. Bell had never heard before. Mrs. McGregor seized a kitten in each hand, put them safely back in the basket and shut the lid. Mrs. Bell snatched Minka up and held her tight in spite of her struggles. But she wasn't like a kitten any more, she was like a little demon. She dug all her twenty claws hard into Mrs. Bell, and they really hurt . . . and her growls changed to a most extraordinary sound . . . exactly like the chattering of a monkey. Strangest of all, her eyes no longer looked blue, but *red*.

'Oh dear,' said Mrs. Bell, 'I don't know how to apologise . . . I've *never* seen her behave like this . . .'

'What a shame,' said Mrs. McGregor. 'I did so hope she'd like Chula and Gumbie. . . . Perhaps, in time, when she's got over the first shock . . .'

'Oh, I do hope so,' said Mrs. Bell. 'They're so sweet.' But she didn't *feel* very hopeful. After all, she hadn't even touched the kittens, to give Minka an excuse for being jealous. The mere *sight* of them had driven her into a frenzy of rage.

It was not till quite a time after Mrs. McGregor had taken Chula and Gumbie back to her own flat that Minka calmed down and became her ordinary size again. The last part to flatten down was that bottle-brush tail. It went down bit by bit, almost like slowly shutting an umbrella. Even then she wasn't quite her ordinary self. She did *not* say she was sorry to Mrs. Bell though, for the first time in her life, she had scratched her quite severely. She was sulky and suspicious and kept peering under beds and cupboards as if she thought those *horrible* creatures might be lurking under them. It was a full hour before she was confident and carefree again.

Mrs. Bell said despairingly to Mrs. Silver:

'If she behaves like that to two visiting kittens, however will she treat one who comes to *live* here? . . . I wonder if I should write to Mrs. Grey and say it's too dangerous even to risk having the other.'

But Mrs. Silver said:

'Mightn't it only have been because they were Siamese? You told me how rude she was to her own brother and sister.'

Mrs. Bell brightened.

'I never thought of that . . . Why, Mrs. McGregor's were brother and sister. *And* chocolate-points! *And* with straight tails and no squints! She must have thought they were Macaroon and Sapphire daring to come *here*.'

She felt more hopeful again, since Minka could not possibly mistake an ordinary marmalade kitten for any of her relations. A few days later, she felt more hopeful still. She saw Chula and Gumbie out in the garden square with Mrs. McGregor. And one of the kittens was actually playing with Whisky, the white tomboy cat with one blue eye and one green one. So Siamese *could* make friends with strangers!

'Which kitten is it, the boy or the girl?' she asked Mrs. McGregor.

'That's Chula,' said Mrs. McGregor. 'She's much bolder and more adventurous than her brother. Gumbie's very shy and still a little frightened of Whisky. Why don't you bring Minka out in the square? Then she might get used to other cats.'

'I can't take her out till her knitted coat is ready,' said Mrs. Bell. 'All the ready-made coats were so much too big for her that I've had to order one to be made to measure.'

'Chula and Gumbie don't need coats,' said Mrs. McGregor. 'They were used to going out of doors before I had them. But I know that Minka will need a coat till the winter's over because she has lived indoors since she was born. What fun her first outing will be!'

'I'm looking forward to it,' said Mrs. Bell. 'Oh, I do hope she'll like playing in the square as much as Chula and Gumbie do.'

But she was pretty sure that never, never would she see the charming sight of *three* chocolate-points playing together in the garden.

10

ONE MORNING, Minka's knitted coat arrived. It looked like a doll's sleeveless jumper and was made of fawn-coloured wool with a blue polo collar to match her eyes. Mrs. Bell had also bought a blue silk harness and lead for her. It was quite a business getting Minka's slim brown legs through the holes in the coat but at last it was on and very smart she looked. It was harder still to fasten the lead because Minka kept rolling over and trying to bite it.

Having first made sure from her window that Chula and Gumbie weren't in the square (since she didn't want to risk another dreadful scene), Mrs. Bell carried Minka downstairs and across the road. Minka looked about her inquisitively and her sensitive ears twitched at all the new noises in the street. She was interested but a trifle nervous. To get into the square garden, Mrs.

Bell had to unlock a gate. So she shifted Minka under one arm and put one hand through the loop of the lead in case she should try to run away and put the big key in the lock with her other hand.

Just as she was turning the key—it was rather stiff— a boy on a bicycle rang his bell very loud. She felt Minka struggling under her arm, and the next moment she knew she wasn't there any more. She held tight to the lead so that she shouldn't run away. But she couldn't feel any weight on the end of the lead. She looked down and, to her horror, saw she was holding nothing but a lead and an empty woollen jacket. And there, scampering away up the street, with her tail in the air and fluffed up in a bottle-brush, was Minka, dressed in nothing but her own cream fur and brown stockings.

Mrs. Bell only caught her just in time to prevent her jumping off the pavement right in front of an approaching car. Tucking Minka under her coat, Mrs. Bell carried her into the gardens and locked the gate safely behind them. Then she put on the jacket and harness that Minka had struggled out of like a little eel and tried to make her walk on the grass. But Minka wouldn't walk. She lay down and seemed to think it fun to be pulled along like that, like a child's toy. So, as it was safe in the square and there were no other cats about, Mrs. Bell tried to make her walk on her own without her lead and harness. But Minka didn't want to do that either. She seemed frightened by the strange open space. In- stead of playing with the fallen leaves as Chula and

Gumbie did, she crouched down quite still, shivering all over and mewing plaintively. She obviously didn't like the garden one little bit.

So Mrs. Bell picked her up, put on the harness again, tucked her very tight under one arm and went out into the street again. She was going to take her straight home but suddenly Minka began to purr. It seemed that she quite liked being out of doors provided her mistress carried her. Mrs. Bell carried her like that down several streets, avoiding the main road so that the noise of the buses shouldn't frighten her. Minka obviously enjoyed this new experience. Several people stopped and said, 'Oh, what a darling kitten!' and Minka accepted their admiration most graciously. But when a little boy said, 'Look, Mummy, there's a baby monkey in a woolly jumper,' she looked deeply offended.

After that Mrs. Bell quite often took her for walks. That is to say, Mrs. Bell took the walks, for out of doors Minka refused to set paw to the ground. She preferred to sit on Mrs. Bell's shoulder, looking very proud and pleased with herself like a little Siamese princess perched high up on a royal elephant, accepting homage from the passers-by. But, alas, when she saw another cat of *any* breed, she snarled and swore and fluffed up her tail. At intervals, a postcard would come from Mrs. Grey in Rye to say that the marmalade kitten was growing stronger and livelier and handsomer every week. And, at last, it was the end of November and he was pronounced ready to leave his mother. Would Mrs.

Bell come down to Rye, stay the night with Mrs. Grey and fetch him back to London?

Mrs. Bell laid her plans very carefully. She decided to go on a Saturday and come back on a Sunday, so that she could leave Minka in charge of Alice who did not go to her office at week-ends. It was the first time she had been away for a night since Minka had arrived. That would be one shock for Minka and then would come the much bigger one of the new kitten. So she and Alice worked out a plot to spare Minka's feelings as much as possible. When Mrs. Bell arrived home, she would ring the street-door bell instead of using her latchkey as usual. Alice would then go down, let her in, take charge of the cat-basket and wait five minutes. Then after Mrs. Bell had gone up to the flat, and made a great fuss of Minka, Alice would arrive with the cat-basket as if it were *she* who had brought the newcomer, and very, very cautiously, with each of them taking charge of one, they would introduce the young kitten to the older one.

II

'THIS IS where Mamma lives,' said Mrs. Grey, stopping in front of a little red house in a steep, cobbled street. 'Look through the window and perhaps you'll see her . . . and *him*.'

Sure enough, in front of the fire, lay a fine large tortoise-shell cat with two kittens nestled against her, all of them fast asleep. But both kittens were black-and-white. Then Mrs. Bell saw something moving. Trying to climb up the big fireguard was a beautifully marked pure marmalade kitten. He didn't get very far because he was none too certain on his legs and kept slipping down again. But he kept trying again with great determination.

'Oh, I *do* like him!' said Mrs. Bell. 'He's such an enterprising kitten, as well as being so handsome.' Without any disloyalty to Minka, she knew at once that this was a little cat no one could help loving. She hoped and prayed Minka would come to feel the same way. But she had all too much reason to fear she wouldn't.

When Mrs. Bell went inside and was introduced to the marmalade kitten, she liked him more than ever. He couldn't have been more friendly. He climbed up on to her lap (it was easier for him than the fireguard because her skirt gave him a better foothold) and stalked about on her knees, with his little pointed tail sticking up like a flag. Being only six weeks old, he was of course a good deal smaller than Minka, though nothing like as much smaller as he would have been compared to an ordinary cat of nearly six months. But after her sleek, elegant stream-lining, this kitten was just a roly-poly bundle of striped fur. Everything about him seemed to be round except his defiant little pointed tail. He had a round innocent pansy face, round blue eyes and a plump barrel of a body. His round paws (already far larger than Minka's oval ones) were absurdly too big for him. He kept stumbling over them like someone wearing shoes several sizes too large. His purr, on the other hand, was several sizes too small. Compared to Minka's, it was a mere whisper. He couldn't manage it very well either; it kept fading out and having to be wound up again. And after Minka's imperious yowl, his mew was a faint squeak. But his colouring was glorious. He was pure marmalade, without a single white hair, beautifully marked with deep orange stripes on a back-ground of tawny gold. He was such a perfect sun-kitten that Mrs. Bell almost christened him Phoebus on the spot. Yet somehow, she *knew* that was not his right name.

Mamma and the two other kittens woke up and came to investigate. The marmalade jumped down and began to play with his black-and-white sisters. It was obvious that, unlike Minka, he was devoted to them. Mamma sniffed Mrs. Bell very carefully and examined her with a very thoughtful expression. She was evidently asking herself:

77

'Is this a person to whom I can really trust my beautiful golden son?' At last she seemed to be satisfied, gave a gracious purr and turned round to tell her children: 'Gently with each other's tails, now.'

Mrs. Bell felt it was almost cruel to break up such a happy family. But, fortunately, there were no painful scenes. Mamma gave her son a good wash and obviously added some good advice as she did his ears. Mrs. Bell had left the comfortably lined cat-basket open in the hopes the marmalade kitten would decide to investigate it. To her delight, he clambered into it on his own and did not seem to mind when she shut the lid.

As she carefully carried the basket back to Mrs. Grey's house, she heard one or two squeaky little mews, but that was all.

She and Mrs. Grey opened the basket in the kitchen, having made sure both doors were shut and Mrs. Grey's two cats out in the garden. A saucer of warm milk was ready waiting. They lifted the lid and there sat the marmalade kitten looking a little puzzled but not at all frightened. Mrs. Bell picked him up and put him on the floor. He stood quite still, with his little legs splayed out and his tail in the air. Then he smelt the milk, staggered up to the saucer and began to lap. He splashed a good deal, but it was obvious he had learnt to lap properly.

'Isn't he a darling?' said Mrs. Grey. 'Look, he's making himself at home already.'

There was a scratching at the garden door.

'Oh dear,' said Mrs. Grey. 'That's Boudy wanting to

come and see what's going on. Do you think I dare let her in? She is very gentle . . . but I don't want to frighten him.'

'Let him finish his milk,' said Mrs. Bell. 'Then I'll hold him and you let Boudy in.'

When Mrs. Grey *did* let Boudy in, the black cat looked much more surprised than the marmalade kitten. She backed towards the garden door, obviously *very* puzzled. It was some time since she had last had kittens and she was sure she hadn't had one *that* colour. But the kitten stalked up to her, staggering slightly because he was so full of milk, and sniffed at her. He obviously knew she wasn't his own Mamma but he seemed to think she might be some kind of relation . . . say an aunt. He gave a friendly little squeak. Boudy went on staring at him in a rather stand-offish way. Then she turned round with great dignity and asked Mrs. Grey to let her out into the garden again. As she did so, she waved her plumy black tail. The kitten simply couldn't resist that tail. He stood on his hind legs and made a bat at it with one of his outsize paws. Mrs. Bell held her breath. But instead of turning and cuffing him for his impudence, Boudy forgot her dignity and fairly streaked out into the garden. The kitten, who had lost his balance and tumbled over backwards, looked very bewildered when he got himself on all fours again. He obviously wondered where that gorgeous tail had vanished to.

Mrs. Grey laughed as she shut the garden door.

'He's as bold as brass,' she said admiringly. 'That tiny thing . . . not an hour since he left his mother . . . and already he's cheeking Boudy . . . Oh, I'm sure there'll be no trouble with Minka. He's so friendly, they'll be playing together in no time.'

Mrs. Bell would have liked to think so. But she knew Minka better than Mrs. Grey did. However, it was no good looking on the dark side.

'It won't be *his* fault if they don't,' she said.

At that moment, the front-door bell rang.

'Bother!' said Mrs. Grey. 'I'll have to answer it. But I'll send whoever it is away. We must get the kitten thoroughly used to you before you take him back tomorrow and we don't want other people bewildering him.'

She ran out into the passage so quickly that she forgot to shut the kitchen door. Mrs. Bell heard the front door open. The next moment there was a heavy scampering noise in the passage. Then, to her horror, into the kitchen bounded an enormous black DOG! She nearly screamed. She was stooping down to snatch up the kitten when the most extraordinary thing happened. She felt the kitten's tiny back arch under her hand and heard a small, but businesslike snarl. In the same second, she realised there was no other sound in the kitchen. She looked round and there was the big black dog, sitting on its haunches and looking almost as frightened as she felt herself. She was so surprised that she took her hand off the kitten's back and stood staring at both of them. The kitten arched its back, fluffed up its baby fur and bristled its infant whiskers. And out of its open pink mouth came the most menacing swears. The huge black dog, who could have made one mouthful of it, did not attempt to advance; instead, it cowered on its haunches and even shifted back a little. It was the marmalade kitten who took a step forward, still hissing and swearing. And as Mrs. Bell stood holding her breath, the great black Labrador stood up, turned round and slunk out of the kitchen with its tail between its legs.

'You little wonder!' she said, picking it up and cuddling it. The kitten relaxed and snuggled up to her. Though it had been so astonishingly brave, it was obviously relieved not to have to be any more.

Mrs. Grey and her friend who owned the black Labrador came into the kitchen.

'We saw it all from the passage,' said Mrs. Grey.

'I knew Paula wouldn't *hurt* it,' said Paula's mistress. 'She's used to cats and very good-natured. But I was terrified she would frighten the poor little thing.'

'Poor little thing nothing,' said Mrs. Grey. 'That kitten's as brave as a lion.'

'He certainly is,' said Paula's mistress. 'Paula, you

great coward, letting yourself be put to flight by a baby one-twentieth your size. Come in and make friends.'

But Paula preferred to stay outside and Mrs. Bell was secretly relieved when her owner, after having stroked and admired the marmalade kitten, took her home. The kitten had had quite enough excitement for one day.

Mrs. Grey made some tea and she and Mrs. Bell took the tray into the drawing-room and had tea in front of a lovely blazing wood fire. The November evening was getting chilly and the wind from the sea blew down the cobbled streets of Rye. But inside, with the curtains drawn and the fire flickering on their faces as they made themselves hot buttered toast, nothing could have been cosier. The marmalade kitten curled up on Mrs. Bell's lap and went to sleep.

'What are you going to call him?' asked Mrs. Grey. 'A kitten of such noble spirit should have a very special name. I have never seen anything so brave as the way he faced up to Paula.'

'Yes, indeed,' said Mrs. Bell, feeling very proud of her new kitten's spirit. 'I think I shall call him Cœur-de-Lion after King Richard the lion-hearted. I believe *he* had red-gold hair too.' She ran a finger over the fluffy coat that felt so warm and silky after the cool chiffon texture of Minka's. And how soft and pudgy his body seemed after her firm, compact one.

'I think that is a splendid name,' said Mrs. Grey. 'Though perhaps Cœur-de-Lion is a little overwhelming for such a tiny thing, also difficult to call in a hurry.'

'It will be his official name,' explained Mrs. Bell. 'I shall call him Curdy for short.'

'Splendid,' said Mrs. Grey. 'I like Curdy as a name. When I was a child, I was very fond of a book called *The Princess and Curdie* . . . Why, it is just right . . . For Minka really is a princess, isn't she?'

Mrs. Bell sighed. 'Oh, I *do* hope all goes well,' she said. 'I love Minka *so* much . . . I couldn't bear her to be hurt or jealous. Yet I already love Curdy too.'

At that moment Boudy and her grown-up son Torky asked to come in and sit by the fire. They had been playing in the garden all the afternoon and now they wanted milk, warmth and a snooze. Almost at once, Curdy woke up. *He* was in the mood for a game. He tried to lure Boudy and Torky into one, making little rushes at them and dabbing at their tails with his outsize paws that looked like fur boxing-gloves. But the grown-up cats were not in the mood. They spoke a little crossly to him and went and settled on the backs of armchairs too high for him to reach.

'Oh dear, this must be the time of *his* evening romp,' said Mrs. Bell. 'I'm afraid he misses his mother and sisters.'

Mrs. Grey threw him a big ball of wool and he scrabbled

with it and undid a lot and wound himself up in the strands. Then suddenly he fell asleep again, clutching the ball to him as if it were another kitten.

Mrs. Bell knew he was bound to be a little homesick the first night without Mamma's warm flank to lie against and his sisters to cuddle up to. So she took him up to bed with her. She waited to see where he would settle. It didn't take Curdy long to decide. In a minute, he had curled himself up on her *right* shoulder and was purring them both to sleep with his funny whisper of a purr. As she dozed off, Mrs. Bell thought: 'How strange he should choose the right! I wonder if he can possibly guess that my left shoulder is reserved for Minka and always will be.' She fell asleep wondering whether she would ever do so with a sun-kitten on one shoulder and a moon-kitten on the other.

12

THE NEXT morning, Mrs. Bell started off for London, as soon as she had been to church. She wanted to have as long as possible for the ordeal that lay ahead. The fact that it was Sunday and Alice would be in the flat all day would make things easier. If Minka resisted Curdy's arrival *too* fiercely (Mrs. Bell had no rosy dreams that she would welcome him with open paws), Alice would be able to look after Curdy and make him feel at home. Mrs. Bell knew that her first duty would have to be to soothe Minka.

Curdy slept peacefully in his basket all through the train journey. But when Mrs. Bell got into a taxi and put the basket on the seat beside her, much squeaking and jumping about went on inside. So, making sure the windows were shut, she let Curdy out. He was in high spirits after his long sleep and full of curiosity. He stood up on his hind legs in her lap, boxing the window with his big paws, and squeaking with excitement at all the new sights and sounds. When the taxi drew up outside her house, she had quite a business catching him and shutting him safely in his basket again.

The moment she rang the bell, Alice came running down the six flights to open the door, as arranged.

'I can hardly wait to see him,' she said, as she took the basket. 'Is he nice?'

'He's adorable. But quick, tell me, how is Minka?'

'She's been very good. But she's missed you dreadfully. She keeps looking for you all over the flat and yowling. She wouldn't sleep with me but went and curled up all by herself on your bed.'

'Oh dear, I must go to her at once. Give me a little time to pet her and comfort her before you bring *him* up. Perhaps it will be best to introduce them in *your* sitting-room. It might soften the first shock if she thinks he belongs to you.'

As she climbed the last flight, Mrs. Bell heard a well-known voice. The moment she opened the door and stooped to pick up her suitcase, something bounded on to her shoulder and purred loud and deep in her ear. Minka had recognised her step on the stairs and had been waiting just inside the door. Mrs. Bell sat down on the stairs and hugged her and stroked her. Minka simply couldn't make enough fuss of her. But every now and then she would break off her loud purring and pat Mrs. Bell's cheek with one slender brown paw and squint at her with great reproachful blue eyes, as if to say: 'How *could* you leave me like that?' And Mrs. Bell looked back at her so intently that she felt as if she were becoming cross-eyed too. She also felt dreadfully guilty.

All too soon, she heard Alice coming up the outer stairs. Hurriedly she carried Minka into Alice's sitting-room. Minka looked extremely suspicious. Her forehead

wrinkled into its worried frown as if to say: 'Why aren't
we going into one of *our* rooms?'

The moment Alice entered with the cat-basket she
sprang off Mrs. Bell's lap and began to paw at it and sniff
it. She didn't wait for the squeak that came from inside
before her back went up and her tail swelled into a bottle-
brush and she began to swear under her breath.

'Oh dear,' said Alice and Mrs. Bell together. 'We must
be prepared for the worst.'

Mrs. Bell snatched Minka up and held her tight, stroking her and saying the most loving things. But the
Siamese remained absolutely tense in her arms, her
muscles hard as whipcord and her brown ears flattened.

'Do you think I *dare* take him out?' whispered
Alice.

'Yes, but hold on to him tight. I've got a good grip on
Minka. I'll turn my back to you.'

Very carefully, Alice lifted Curdy out and held him
safe in her arms. Mrs. Bell turned her back to spare Minka
the first sight of the stranger. But before you could say
knife, Minka had furiously clawed her way up on to Mrs.
Bell's shoulder, scratching her so hard that she loosened
her grip, and streaked down her back on to the floor. Mrs.
Bell swung round and there was Minka crouching on the
carpet with her ears back and the most strange and sinister
sounds coming out of her throat. Curdy, for all his brav-
ery, was obviously frightened. He clung desperately to
Alice, who was holding him safe with both hands. It was
clear that he had never seen such a dreadful fierce animal

87

... it wasn't a dog and didn't seem to be a *cat* ... in all his short life.

Even to those who knew her, Minka seemed to have suddenly changed into a wild jungle stranger. She was creeping very slowly inch by inch across the carpet on her belly, staring at Curdy as if she were trying to hypnotise him and, though her mouth was open, she was making very little noise. What sound she did make was more like a low, hoarse crooning. This quietness and slow, intent slinking forward were far more alarming than her furious snarling at Chula and Gumbie. That had been plain, uncontrollable rage but this disciplined tenseness was far more sinister. Before she could spring, Mrs. Bell swept her up, carried her out of the room and shut the door. For a moment or two, Minka was almost hysterical, clawing and struggling. After Mrs. Bell had taken her into her own sitting-room she gradually calmed down. It took a great deal of stroking and loving talk before she did, and even then Minka would not give even the tiniest purr. But at last she leant her head against Mrs. Bell's shoulder and lay there with her eyes half-closed, as if too exhausted

to care any more. Even then, at intervals, she would begin to mutter and chatter to herself in Siamese. She was
like a person who has almost decided to forgive and forget
and then remembers how cruelly her feelings have been
outraged and begins to go over it all again in her mind
and grow angry once more.

It was already long past Minka's lunch-time. Mrs.
Bell thought some food might be the best possible thing to
appease her. So she took her into the kitchen and cut up
some rabbit for her. Usually Minka was so greedy that
she would keep pushing her nose into the plate before her
food was cut up and risking getting her whiskers chopped
off with the scissors. But, though rabbit was her very
favourite food and she usually growled with excitement
when she smelt it, today she showed not the slightest
interest. She stood silent and sulky at the other end of the
kitchen while Mrs. Bell was cutting the rabbit up. Even
when the plate was put down in front of her nose, she
turned away her head and wouldn't touch it.

At that moment Mrs. Bell heard Alice call out: 'Curdy
. . . you naughty kitten . . . come back.' It was too late.
Bouncing along the passage at full speed came Curdy,
right into the kitchen. He had smelt that rabbit and nothing would stop him. Minka gave one low growl, but it
was as if she were too proud to assert herself. She backed
away, looking at the marmalade kitten with bitter hatred,
but not trying to attack him. And, right under her very
nose, Curdy calmly ate as many pieces of rabbit as he
could before Alice picked him up and carried him off.

Hungry as he was, it wouldn't have been good for him to have any more for already his small sides were almost bursting. But he squealed most indignantly when he was removed from the rabbit and even gave a little growl. It was evident *he* had quite recovered his spirits.

Poor Minka had not. First, her feelings had been outraged, now her dignity had been insulted. Even if she did not want it herself, to have *her* rabbit snatched off *her* plate under her very nose by this revolting little intruder was more than she could bear. She looked at Mrs. Bell so coldly and reproachfully that she could hardly endure it.

Yet Minka was obviously curious, as one can be about something one intensely dislikes. Very cautiously she began to prowl up the stairs, in the direction Alice had gone.

Mrs. Bell followed her, warily. Unknown to her, Alice had taken Curdy up to show him his tray which she had placed beside Minka's while Mrs. Bell was in Rye. Mrs. Bell caught Minka up and held her tight at a safe distance. Alice gently dumped Curdy on his tray. But he wouldn't use it. He just scattered the sawdust about with his paws. Then he jumped out and staggered over to Minka's, stepped into it and squatted down in it. He had a positively smug look on his face as he used it and then industriously tidied the sawdust. Mrs. Bell nearly had to laugh but she did not dare. She was too conscious of Minka stiff with anger in her arms and beginning to snarl menacingly.

'Quick, Alice, take him away,' she called and Alice had only just time to vanish with Curdy and shut the door, before Minka had sprung to the ground spitting with rage. Mrs. Bell said through the door:

'Whatever you do, don't open it, till I've taken Minka downstairs. I daren't even let her set eyes on him again today. Take his tray into your room and feed him there too. Oh dear, things are even worse than I expected.'

Alice called back:

'Don't worry, Mrs. Bell. You look after Minka and I'll look after Curdy. I think it's horrid of her to be so spiteful. He's such a baby. And he is longing to make friends with her, in spite of the horrible way she behaved.'

'Still . . . it *was* rather cheek eating her rabbit and using her tray . . .'

'*I* think it was wonderful,' said Alice. 'He's the bravest, funniest, darlingest kitten I ever saw.' And she cooed. '*Aren't* you, Cœur-de-Lion?'

But Mrs. Bell was too concerned with Minka's feelings to stay and argue.

The rest of that Sunday that had begun so cheerfully was anything but happy. However much Mrs. Bell tried to make peace with Minka, Minka refused to be comforted. She coaxed her to eat a little, but nothing would make her purr or play. Even though Curdy was kept well out of sight, Minka kept rushing to the door of Alice's room and swearing under it. When she was shut up with Mrs. Bell, she was alternately moody and almost hysterical. By bedtime Mrs. Bell felt almost hysterical herself and her

91

head ached dreadfully from the nervous strain. Oh, what *had* she done? By bringing home Curdy, she had utterly destroyed her friendship with her beloved Minka. And, tomorrow, Alice wouldn't be there to look after Curdy. The poor little thing would have to be shut up alone like a prisoner, instead of running happily all over the flat. And Mrs. Bell would be left alone with two miserable kittens, one whom she daren't speak to and one who wouldn't speak to her.

Sadly she took Minka up to her bedroom as usual, and propped the door open so that she could get to her tray. But, as she feared, the minute she put her down, Minka streaked round the door and vanished. Mrs. Bell was almost sure she had gone down to the kitchen to spend the night in the old box under the sink where she always retired when she was in low spirits. It was no good following her and coaxing her back. Minka obviously wanted to be alone and she must respect her wishes. Mrs. Bell undressed quickly and got into bed. She was glad to lay her aching head on the pillow. But, as she turned out the light, she felt lonely and in disgrace. It was the first time for a whole month she had gone to sleep without a kitten on her shoulder.

She hadn't even begun to doze off when a wonderful thing happened. She felt a light weight land noiselessly on her bed. The next moment something crept into the hollow of her left shoulder and snuggled up there purring like a dynamo. It was unmistakably a Siamese purr. She put up her hand and stroked the cool, smooth fur. Minka purred till she nearly choked. It was as if she couldn't be loving enough to make up for her bad temper and for the night Mrs. Bell had been away. Mrs. Bell went to sleep very happily indeed, certain that Minka had forgiven her.

13

IN THE morning Mrs. Bell was wakened by a delicate paw patting her cheek. Her headache had quite gone and there was Minka, still in her most affectionate mood, purring away like mad.

'Everything's going to be all right,' she thought happily.

Alas, she was wrong. A second later, a faint squeak of a mew sounded outside. Minka stopped purring, leapt off the bed and ran out of the room. Mrs. Bell rushed after her, still in her nightdress. Curdy had escaped from Alice's bedroom, while she was having her bath, and was calmly squatting on Minka's tray. This time Minka did not do more than give him one long insulting snarl, then stalked away with great dignity.

When Mrs. Bell went down to give her her breakfast, it was obvious that Minka was deeply offended again. Mrs. Bell felt she was even angrier with *her* than with the marmalade kitten. Not one purr would she give; she walked away coldly when Mrs. Bell tried to stroke her. As soon as she had finished her breakfast, she went and hid under the sink.

As Alice had to go off to work, Mrs. Bell had to pay
some attention to Curdy. She took him up some bread-
and-milk and let him scamper about her sitting-room.
Then she cleaned his tray and put it out beside
Minka's, explaining to him that *this* one was his. She
was fairly sure he understood. Back in her sitting-room,
he had a wonderful time, getting into her waste-paper
basket, falling over with it and chasing the bits of paper.

Then she heard Mrs. Silver arriving. She didn't dare
take Curdy down to introduce him. She shut him up in
her sitting-room and went downstairs. But someone had
already gone to meet Mrs. Silver. The minute she
appeared, Minka had rushed into her arms and there she
was chattering and growling away, obviously complaining
of the *dreadful* thing Mrs. Bell had done.

It was not till Mrs. Silver came up and said that Minka
was safely asleep in the dining-room that she was able to
be introduced to Curdy. Just as she was stroking him
and admiring him, he suddenly jumped out of her arms
and dashed towards the banisters. Before they could stop
him, he had fallen through them, a good ten feet, into the
passage below. Mercifully there was a soft carpet and he
fell on his feet. He was so well padded that he bounced
like a rubber ball.

They rushed downstairs. He wasn't hurt a bit, but he
did look very startled.

'Poor little thing,' said Mrs. Silver. 'He must have
given himself a dreadful fright.'

Not a bit of it. When Mrs. Bell took him upstairs, he immediately made for the banisters and was only just prevented from doing it all over again . . . on purpose.

In the afternoon, when Mrs. Silver had gone home, Mrs. Bell realised she just couldn't keep both kittens shut up. Nor could she let them roam about the flat in case Curdy damaged himself or was attacked by Minka. She decided to risk having both in her sitting-room, where at least she could prevent serious trouble.

Minka snarled and cuffed at him whenever he came near her, but did not actually attack him. He *was* a little frightened, but he stood his ground and did not run away. He obviously felt safe as long as Mrs. Bell was there.

As she really had to do some work that morning, she sat down at her typewriter. Curdy forgot all about Minka in his excitement at this wonderful new toy. He jumped on to Mrs. Bell's lap, then on to her desk and tried to type too with his boxing-glove paws. Discouraged from this, he began to chew up a page of manuscript. At last, in the sudden way kittens do, he felt sleepy. Mrs. Bell dared not let him curl up on her lap for fear of hurting Minka's feelings. So she gently deposited him on the hearthrug, and in a moment he was fast asleep.

Minka was now sitting in the furthest corner of the room with her paws folded under her, squinting at the kitten with cold dislike. But from the way she was blinking, it was obvious she was getting sleepy too. Mrs. Bell picked her up, put her on her lap and fondled her. Minka was completely unresponsive and promptly jumped off. At last she settled down in her basket, which she had not used for weeks, preferring to sit on Mrs. Bell's lap or behind her on the chair when she was writing, and went to sleep. But her attitude and expression showed that, even in her sleep, she was sulking. She woke up before Curdy did and began to play, rather half-heartedly, with a ping-pong ball. She did not, as usual, ask Mrs. Bell to come and throw it for her. And she was treating the ball very strangely. She would give it a tap or two, then suddenly crouch down and begin to swear and growl at it. It was obvious she was remembering her grievances and working them off on the ping-pong ball as if it were the hated rival.

Mrs. Bell could no longer concentrate on her book. So she wrote a long letter to Mrs. Grey telling her all that had happened since Curdy's arrival and ending up: 'I fear there seems no hope of Minka's *ever* making peace with him.'

When she went to post this, she took Minka with her. Partly because she daren't leave her alone with Curdy: partly to show Minka she was First Lady as she had always been and had special privileges, such as being taken for walks on her shoulder, which Curdy did not share. Minka merely perched there, cold and aloof, without a single purr or even an attempt to make conversation. People who stopped to admire her in her knitted coat with the blue collar got no encouragement either. She merely squinted at them disdainfully.

As soon as they got home, she flew upstairs the moment Mrs. Bell had removed her jacket, to see if That Creature was still in the sitting-room. It was . . . and, worst of all . . . it was actually curled up on Minka's own favourite chair . . . the one at Mrs. Bell's desk. This was too much for her feelings. Mrs. Bell was only just in time to rescue Curdy from a snarling, spitting fury with all its brown claws out. Without thinking what she was doing, she gave Minka a hard slap . . . the first she had ever given her. The moment she had done it, she realised it was the very worst thing she could have done. It would only make Minka more jealous and resentful than ever. Minka fled from the room, screaming, and would not come near Mrs. Bell for the rest of the day.

However, that night, when Curdy was once more shut up in Alice's bedroom, Minka did creep to her usual place to sleep. But not one purr did she give. She lay all night on Mrs. Bell's shoulder with her head turned away, as still and dumb as a stuffed toy.

The next day, Tuesday, things were no better. Mrs. Bell's only comfort was that Curdy, at least, wasn't unhappy. It was astonishing how gay and cheeky and unsnubbable that marmalade kitten was. He hadn't a touch of nerves or temperament. He was friendly to everyone and took it for granted everyone would be friendly to him. Not only was he not in the least cross with Minka for being so horrid to him . . . for she still growled whenever he came near her . . . but he actually cheeked her and tried to play with her. Once he thrust his golden face right into her saucer of milk just when she was going to drink from it. She slapped him hard and he was slightly taken aback. But two hours later, he crept up behind her and actually pulled her kinky tail. Naturally he got an even harder slap and Minka swore so loud and so long that she was quite exhausted. And then, just as she was sitting in front of the fire, washing herself to restore her shattered nerves, he actually jumped down from the top of a cupboard and landed right on top of her. She was so startled, she didn't even swear. She just gave a great leap and sent him sprawling on his back.

However, he did at last seem to grasp that this majestic person did not want to play with him and went off to amuse himself on his own. Mrs. Bell looked thoughtfully at Minka, as, resuming her interrupted wash, she sat by the fire, deliberately ignoring her
mistress. She did
not dare go and
make a fuss of
her. A change
had come over
Minka in the last
two days. Not
only was she icy
with Mrs. Bell,
but she seemed to

have grown older. True, she was nearly six months old now, but she was still a kitten and, until Mrs. Bell had gone to Rye, she had frisked about as wildly as Curdy himself. Now she seemed suddenly to have decided to become a grown-up cat . . . and a very staid, aloof grown-up cat at that. Mrs. Bell felt very sad. She longed for her mischievous, affectionate Minka and knew it was all her fault that she had vanished. Though Minka still disliked the marmalade kitten intensely, it was obvious that she felt far far more bitter towards Mrs. Bell.

14

AT INTERVALS during that Tuesday, a plaintive squeaky mew would make Mrs. Bell rush out to see what trouble Curly had got himself into *now*. Once he had got into a big box of biscuits and couldn't scrabble out. Another time he had overturned one of his favourite waste-paper baskets on himself and was squeaking piteously inside his wicker cage. A third time, rolling empty milk-bottles about the kitchen floor, he had somehow got his paw stuck inside one. It was Minka's sharp ears that usually heard the squeak first and warned Mrs. Bell with their twitching. But *she* naturally made no attempt to go to his aid, though she noticed jealously that Mrs. Bell promptly dropped whatever she was doing to go and see what was the matter.

In the afternoon, Mrs. Bell had both kittens up in her sitting-room again. Minka sat by the fire, more aloof and grown-up than ever. Curdy was playing happily with *her* ping-pong ball. She began to watch him, first resentfully, then with faint curiosity. Suddenly the ball came rolling towards her and she instinctively put out a paw to pat it back. Then, before she had touched the ball, she hastily withdrew the paw, turned her back and began, very deliberately, to wash herself. Her face wore a dignified, disapproving expression that reminded Mrs. Bell irresistibly of Victoria. It said so clearly: 'Such childish games are beneath our notice. We are *not* amused.'

That evening, Minka ate her dinner in the same stony silence and, the moment she had finished, stalked out of the kitchen and went upstairs. Mrs. Bell began to cook her own dinner. Just as a saucepan was about to boil, she heard an agonised yowling coming right from the top of the house. It was definitely Minka's voice raised not in anger but in pain or fright. Leaving the saucepan to boil over, Mrs. Bell rushed upstairs. The yowling was coming from the attic, two flights up. Had the door banged behind Minka and shut her in . . . or, worse still, caught her tail? No, the door was wide open. And just inside it stood Minka, staring down the stairs and mewing piteously, exactly like a cat who has climbed too high up a tree and is frightened to come down again.

'But, Minka dear,' said Mrs. Bell, 'you've been up and down those stairs dozens of times . . . you can't be frightened of them.'

'I a-a-m,' wailed Minka. And she actually shivered. Mrs. Bell walked up the second flight and stooped down to stroke her encouragingly. As she did so, she jumped on Mrs. Bell's shoulder. It was clear what she wanted . . . to be carried down those stairs, just as Mrs. Bell used to carry her weeks ago when she first arrived. As they reached the bottom step, for the first time for nearly two whole days, Minka purred.

The same thing happened again at bedtime. When Mrs. Bell was half undressed, she heard the same frantic yowling from the floor above. When she went out on to the landing, there was Minka standing at the top of the attic stairs, pretending she hadn't the faintest idea how to get down again. Once again Mrs. Bell had to go up and bring her down on her shoulder. This time Minka's purr was positively triumphant.

As Minka curled up on her shoulder, more trustingly than the night before, but still with a certain reserve, Mrs. Bell reflected that the Siamese character was quite extraordinary. Minka not only had violent and sensitive feelings but she evidently thought things out. She had noticed that Mrs. Bell rushed to Curdy's aid every time he mewed plaintively. So she had wanted to find out if Mrs. Bell still loved her enough to do the same for her. To do so she had pretended to be a nervous kitten again. In fact she had behaved exactly like a human child who is jealous of a new baby.

On Wednesday, Minka was in a decidedly better mood. She did no more than give Curdy a light cuff when she ran into him and once went so far as to sniff at his golden coat. She even seemed to decide it did not smell *too* dreadful for she had another sniff. Just as Mrs. Bell's hopes were beginning to rise, Curdy himself went and spoiled everything. Like many cheerful, easy-going characters who ignore other people's bad temper, he never noticed what *made* them cross. He hadn't one atom of tact. And, just when Minka was delicately approaching her tray to use it, he deliberately jumped into it and used it himself. Minka was furious. There was nothing for her to do but use his, which was perfectly clean. She sat on the sawdust with such an expression of martyred dignity that Mrs. Bell found it terribly hard not to laugh.

However, she decided it would be wiser to banish Curdy from her sitting-room that morning and let Minka reign supreme. She sent Curdy off to help Mrs. Silver make the beds which he loved to do, especially if he could get himself made into them so that all the sheets and blankets had to be untucked again. Minka was pleased at this attention and, for the first time since Curdy's arrival, took her old place behind Mrs. Bell on the desk chair. She showed how worthy she was to be a writer's cat by not pawing her pen or pulling papers off the desk, and Mrs. Bell actually managed to get a little work done. But, just as she was beginning her third page, the door burst open and in came Mrs. Silver, looking quite pale.

'Do please come at once,' she said. 'He's had a dreadful fall . . . and I'm afraid this time he really *is* hurt.'

'Whatever happened?' asked Mrs. Bell as she hurried downstairs with Mrs. Silver.

'I was washing up in the kitchen and couldn't see him anywhere. I went out, to make sure he wasn't in mischief. I heard him mew from somewhere high up. There he was, looking through the banisters outside the attic. The next minute, he fell right through . . . from two whole floors up and landed right on his poor little head in the passage. I'm afraid he's unconscious.'

Together they stared at the pathetic little heap of red-gold fur that lay in the passage, unmoving. True, the carpet was thick and soft but he had fallen from such a height, with nothing to break his fall. Mrs. Bell's heart turned over. She could hardly bear to go up and touch the limp little body. Then suddenly the heap of fur moved. It staggered to its feet. Then it began to totter slowly round in circles.

'At least he's still alive,' breathed Mrs. Bell.

'I believe he's only stunned himself,' whispered Mrs. Silver.

Mrs. Bell picked him up, sat him on her lap and felt him carefully all over. There were certainly no bones broken. He just looked very dazed and bewildered, but didn't seem to be hurt for he didn't squeak, whatever part of him she gently prodded. Then suddenly he fell fast asleep.

'Best thing for him,' said Mrs. Silver. 'Let's see how he is when he wakes. Maybe it's only a touch of concussion.'

Minka had crept down to see what was going on. For once she did not seem jealous to see Curdy asleep in Mrs. Bell's lap. She even put out her paw and touched him inquisitively. That woke him up. He blinked, yawned and jumped down from Mrs. Bell's lap and walked, rather staggeringly, to his saucer in the kitchen.

'Give him some warm milk,' said Mrs. Bell. 'I think he's still suffering from shock. I'll put some glucose in it, too.'

When Curdy had eagerly lapped up his warm milk and glucose, he didn't seem to be suffering from anything at all. If anything he was livelier than ever. He knocked a milk bottle over and gave it a good long roll. Then he chased his own tail so wildly that he made himself giddy again and had to sit down.

'I don't think there's any need to send for the Vet,' laughed Mrs. Bell.

'No, indeed,' said Mrs. Silver. 'That kitten must be made of indiarubber.'

Just as Curdy got on his feet again, Minka darted forward and boxed his tail. Mrs. Bell had forgotten all about her in the excitement of seeing Curdy recover.

'Gently . . . Minka . . .' she began and stopped. For it was a *playful* box. And the next minute the two kittens were scampering round the kitchen playing hide-and-seek round saucepan-stands and bread-bins and under the 'fridge. Before Mrs. Bell quite took in this marvellous fact, the game stopped as abruptly as it had started. Minka suddenly remembered her dignity and stalked out of the kitchen leaving poor Curdy peeping blankly out of the splendid hiding-place he had just found in the shoe-box.

But Curdy, as usual, couldn't let well alone. Instead of being grateful for her condescension in playing with him even for two minutes, he wanted her to go on. So he chased after her and, of course, got a smart slap and a swear that said, 'Stop pestering me, you little beast.'

15

ON THE Thursday morning, Mrs. Bell took Minka with her when she went to do her shopping and Minka seemed to enjoy her outing. But when they got home, they found Mrs. Silver in a terrible state.

'Curdy's vanished,' she said. 'He can't have followed you out of the flat because he was with me long after you'd gone out and shut the door.'

'Then he must be *somewhere* in the flat,' said Mrs. Bell.

'But I've searched everywhere,' said poor Mrs. Silver. 'In every drawer and every cupboard in case he'd got himself shut in. I've even looked in the 'fridge and the gas-stove.'

'You haven't been out of the flat yourself?'

'Only to take the laundry-basket down to the landing and I *know* he didn't come with me. I was watching the door all the time in case he slipped out.'

'Oh dear, where *can* he have got to?' said Mrs. Bell. And she too searched everywhere she could think of, from the attic to the broom cupboard. Between them they turned the flat upside down, even emptying out drawers in case Curdy had hidden himself under their contents. He wasn't anywhere. Then, to her horror, Mrs. Bell saw that one window was open three inches at the bottom . . . quite enough for even a plump kitten to squeeze through. Outside the window was a broad stone ledge . . . but below the ledge was a sheer drop of at least sixty feet . . . right down into the area. They looked out along the ledge that ran the whole length of the street. It was empty. Mrs. Silver and Mrs. Bell stared at each other in horror. They remembered Curdy's passion for jumping off high places. They remembered his bad fall yesterday that hadn't in the least damped his adventurous spirit. Not even Curdy's indiarubber body would have survived such a fall as this.

Poor Mrs. Silver was nearly crying.

'How *could* I have been so careless? Oh dear, I was always so careful to shut the windows at the bottom. . . . And Mr. Silver was planning to build a cage outside on the ledge so they could both go out safely and sit there in the summer.'

'I'm sure it wasn't your fault,' said Mrs. Bell. But she was nearly crying herself. She just couldn't bear to go down and look in the area for fear of what she might find there.

'It *was*,' moaned Mrs. Silver. 'I remember now, I was just shaking my duster out of the window and the telephone rang. I *did* shut the window before I answered it, but I couldn't have shut it properly. And I was in a hurry to get the laundry packed up, in case the van came early. I must have run back to put the last things in without making sure the window was fast.'

'Wait a minute,' said Mrs. Bell. 'Was Curdy with you when you were doing the laundry?'

'He was at first . . . But he must have wandered off while I was making out the list . . . He certainly wasn't in the room when I strapped the basket up. He *must* have come in here . . .' And she looked miserably at the window. She had shut it now. At least Minka would be safe. But poor little Curdy . . .

'I've an idea,' cried Mrs. Bell suddenly. 'It may be a forlorn hope, but it's worth trying!'

And she tore out of the room, down the stairs, out of the flat and on to the landing, followed by Mrs. Silver. There stood the big laundry-basket. And stooping over it was the van-man (the caretaker had let him in at the street door as usual) just about to hoist it on his shoulders and carry it away . . .

'Wait . . . wait,' Mrs. Bell almost screamed. Hurriedly she undid the straps and began scattering towels and pillow-cases over the landing. Then, under a sheet, she felt a warm lump. She pulled back the sheet, and there snuggled comfortably inside it, lay Curdy, fast asleep.

'You bad, bad kitten to give us such a fright,' said Mrs. Bell and Mrs. Silver. But they were so delighted to find him safe, that they fussed and petted him instead of scolding him.

After all the excitement, Mrs. Bell went into the kitchen to unpack her shopping-basket. She found Minka sitting there sedately, washing herself. Minka had taken no part in the search for Curdy though Mrs. Bell was pretty sure she knew what they had been looking for so frantically. When Curdy came bouncing into the kitchen she gave him rather a disgusted look, then ignored him. The minute the basket was empty, Curdy jumped into it, knocked it over and rolled about the floor in it. This was a wonderful new game and he thoroughly enjoyed it. Minka watched him contemptuously, wearing her most grown-up expression that said: 'Little things please little minds.'

Curdy suddenly got bored with his basket and danced away up the passage, leaving the basket lying on its side. Minka glanced up the passage to make sure he was out of sight. Then, very cautiously, she approached the basket and, with an almost absent-minded expression, crouched down inside it. She gave one or two tentative rocks, then made the basket roll a little way. In a minute she too was rolling the basket over and over along the floor and obviously finding it great fun. But, as soon as she saw Curdy coming back, she jumped out of it and pretended she had not the faintest interest in basket-rolling.

That afternoon, Curdy was cheekier than ever. His two adventures and all the petting he had had after them seemed to have gone to his head. He seemed to think there was nothing he couldn't get away with.

When Mrs. Bell had the two kittens up in the room where she worked, Curdy just wouldn't let either of them alone. First he sat in Minka's special place behind Mrs. Bell's back as she tried to write and kept punching her in the back and clawing her jumper. When, to Minka's delight, she firmly banished him and put Minka there instead, he began to tear up papers on her desk. Minka chattered at him and told him not to. He just cheeked her and went on tearing them. Mrs. Bell dumped him firmly on the floor. Minka bounded down and gave him a cuff . . . and he cuffed her back. She turned her back to him, slowly and majestically swishing her tail to show how thoroughly she disapproved of him. But each time it swished, he boxed the kink at the end. Minka swung round on her hind paws, snarled and hit him really hard, with her claws out. Curdy didn't care a bit. He sprang up on the desk and started taking cigarette-ends out of Mrs. Bell's ash-tray and tossing them about all over the paper she was writing on. She didn't dare put him out of the room for fear he got into serious mischief. It was a huge relief at last when he settled down on a chair and went to sleep.

Minka came over, put her paw on Mrs. Bell's knee and began to chatter softly. But Mrs. Bell realised from her expression that, this time, the chatter meant something different. Minka was not complaining of *her* bad behaviour: she was sympathising with her over Curdy's. She seemed to be saying: 'Honestly, I don't know how *we're* going to put up with this tiresome, ill-mannered little ragamuffin!'

16

BEFORE SHE had relaxed even a little towards Mrs. Bell, there were usually two occasions every day when Minka became gay and kittenish again. Once Curdy was safely stowed away in Alice's bedroom, she enjoyed a good romp in Mrs. Bell's before settling down to sleep on her left shoulder. The other time she played, as in the pre-Curdy days, was in the morning while Mrs. Bell was having her bath. Minka always accompanied her into the bathroom and, behind the locked door, forgot all her new dignity. She balanced on the edge of the bath, fishing for the sponge or Mrs. Bell's toes; she pulled the towels off the rail, and skated over the shiny linoleum.

When the bathroom was empty, one of her favourite places to sit was by the hot pipes of the towel-rail. Even Curdy dared not venture into the bathroom when she was sitting there; it was the one room she had managed to keep absolutely private.

So when, on the Friday morning, Mrs. Bell saw Minka crouching half-asleep at one end of the towel-rail, she could hardly believe her eyes when, at the other, she saw Curdy, in the same grown-up, sphinx-like attitude, facing her. Both were perfectly still and silent. Half an hour later

she came down again. The kittens were still crouching there, perfectly still and silent. But each had shifted forward so that their noses were only about a foot apart. The third time she came down, quite a long time later, they were *still* there. But now they had changed ends of the towel-rail and were crouching far apart, as at first, but with their backs to each other. And each kitten was as still and silent as a statue.

This was something entirely new . . . but obviously very important. Some mysterious communication must have passed between them . . . something that could only happen between cats and that even the most cat-loving human being could not understand.

That afternoon, in the study, she wondered if they had established a kind of treaty to leave each other alone. Curdy played quite demurely with a cork on a piece of string at one end of the room; Minka condescended for the first time to play, in his presence, an elaborate game of ping-pong ball, using her delicate paws with almost self-conscious skill as if to mock Curdy's bumble-kitten boxing. After that, they both lay at opposite ends of the hearthrug and went to sleep. They woke up almost simultaneously. Minka sat up, turned her back to him and began to wash. But as she washed, she moved her tail very gently to and fro. And she kept glancing back over her shoulder, as if expecting Curdy to do something. Could she *possibly* be tempting him to play with it? wondered Mrs. Bell. Curdy was obviously wondering the same. Dare he risk it? He tiptoed very cautiously up to her, then, very gently, patted the swaying tail. Nothing happened. He did it again. This time the tail jumped cleverly out of his way, but back it came, luring him to catch it. She let him play with it for quite a while before she got bored, leapt up on a chair and arranged herself to sleep again. But no sooner had she closed her eyes than Curdy, as usual, went too far. He went and jumped up on the same chair.

'Oh, you *idiot*,' said Mrs. Bell under her breath. 'Now you've gone and ruined everything.'

She watched, waiting for the worst. Minka opened her eyes and looked very cross. But she did not snarl. She did not even push him away.

'Oh, *good* Minka,' said Mrs. Bell. 'This is really angelic forbearance.'

Minka squinted at her from the chair and actually gave a short purr, though Curdy was now squeezing right up against her to get himself into a comfortable position. Mrs. Bell held her breath.

Five minutes later she was writing a hurried postcard to Mrs. Grey.

'I can hardly believe it. At this moment, they are both

asleep in the same chair with C de L's head propped against M's flank. VICTORY!'

The next day, alas, proved that Mrs. Bell had exulted too soon. Though the situation had greatly improved, there were many relapses. There were bouts of playing together but they usually ended in Curdy's being tactless, going too far and getting himself snarled at or slapped. However, he discovered one thing that Minka really did like and that was having her ears washed. Curdy did this with intense concentration, keeping his blue eyes tight shut. Minka accepted this attention most graciously but did not return it. This was a pity, for Curdy was a very sketchy washer himself and his ears were beginning to look decidedly grubby inside. But there was still one thing about which Minka was implacable. She couldn't bear Mrs. Bell to pat or stroke Curdy in her presence. She had only to touch him for Minka to hiss. Curdy had plenty of fussing from Mrs. Silver and Alice and from all visitors to the house, for he was universally popular. It was very hard for Mrs. Bell to ignore him when Minka was there, especially when he looked up at her with that puzzled pansy face, obviously *asking* to be stroked too. But she dared not arouse Minka's jealousy. And, of course, there was no question of Curdy's being allowed so much as to put one whisker into her bedroom at night.

However, on the Sunday, Mrs. Bell woke up thinking how wonderfully things had improved since the dreadful scenes of the *last* Sunday. Considering she had only had the two kittens together for a week, she supposed she should be very grateful. She was already so fond of that brave, absurd, tactless Curdy, she couldn't have borne to send him away. Then she noticed that Minka was frantically scratching her ears. Looking into their delicate mauve lining, she saw there was a lot of dark brown stuff in them, in spite of all Curdy's washing.

'To the Vet with *you* tomorrow, my girl,' she said. 'Those ears need a thorough clean-out.'

Later on, when she saw Curdy scratching *his* ears too, and examining their flannel-pink lining that, like his bright pink nose, clashed slightly with his orange fur, she saw there was dark brown stuff in them too.

'Vet for you too, my boy,' she said.

17

ON MONDAY morning, probably because their ears were irritating them, both kittens seemed to be in a very cross mood. When Mrs. Bell brought down the cat-basket to take them to the Vet's, she had the greatest difficulty in getting them into it. And when she shut the lid on a seething tangle of cream and orange fur, the most fearful snarls in two voices and swears in two languages came out of it. She was quite frightened, as she carried the basket down the street, in case a serious fight was going on inside it. Luckily the Vet lived very near and, when she arrived, all was silence in the basket. When she lifted the lid, the tangle had sorted itself out into two kittens packed neat as sardines, each tail at opposite ends. And both were as quiet and unmoving, as if they really were sardines, but luckily both still had their heads on.

The Vet lifted them out and, while Mrs. Bell held Curdy, deftly cleaned out Minka's ears.

'Siamese are so temperamental, we'd better get her over first,' he said.

Gentle as he was, Minka simply hated it. She struggled and clawed and trembled all over, and streams of saliva ran out of her lilac mouth. Poor Curdy watched in dismay, like a child watching another one in the dentist's chair.

But, when it came to his turn, though he obviously didn't like it, he was very brave indeed and only gave an occasional squeak.

'That's a plucky little chap,' said the Vet, 'and, for a Siamese, *she* was pretty good too. They really are more sensitive than other cats.'

'They certainly *are*,' said Mrs. Bell with feeling.

'They make a pretty pair,' said the Vet. 'Get on well together?'

'We-e-ll . . . up to a point,' said Mrs. Bell cautiously.

'Give 'em time . . . they'll be inseparable.'

Mrs. Bell said she was sure she hoped so. She felt anything but hopeful as the Vet, giving them both a stroke, put them back in the basket, both scratching their ears and looking decidedly offended.

'Their ears will sting for a little. Then they'll feel as comfortable as can be and livelier than ever.'

There was no sound from the basket but an occasional 'Ffff', as Mrs. Bell carried it home. The moment she opened the lid in the kitchen, both kittens leapt out and fled from her into the bathroom. She followed them with saucers of milk to cheer them after their ordeal. They wouldn't touch it. They scampered under the bath and peered out at Mrs. Bell with shocked, reproachful faces. They looked as if they would never trust her again.

'Leave them alone and the milk in with them,' said Mrs. Silver. 'They'll soon get over it.'

So Mrs. Bell went upstairs. Half an hour later she came down again. Both saucers were empty but, the moment she came near Curdy and Minka, they rushed to hide under the bath again.

Some time later she returned to the bathroom. The kittens were sitting one each end of the towel-rail, facing each other. No sound came from them, but they were obviously exchanging thoughts. From the way their heads turned for a moment towards her and then turned at once towards each other again, she was sure they were exchanging thoughts about her—and not at all favourable thoughts. Slowly they got up, walked towards each other, and began licking each other's ears. Before they shut in mutual sympathy, the flax-blue eyes in the marmalade face and the aquamarine ones that squinted through the brown mask gave Mrs. Bell one withering glance. It said quite clearly:

'You're perfectly *horrid*! Fancy doing such a thing to *us*! Ugh, how we hate you!'

Mrs. Bell went away feeling utterly in disgrace. It seemed rather hard that the first time Minka and Curdy were in complete agreement, they should have ganged up together against *her*.

However, it was not long before they both came into the kitchen, urgently demanding lunch. It was evident their ears were perfectly comfortable again for they didn't even twitch them. As they seemed to be on such good terms, she risked feeding them together for the first time, though, of course, on separate plates. Minka, greedy as usual, finished first and began to try and eat out of Curdy's too. A slight argument started which seemed to Mrs. Bell to run like this:

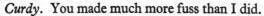

Curdy. Go away, greedy.

Minka. I'm not greedy. I'm twice your age and I need more nourishment.

Curdy. I'm growing so fast, I need every scrap I can get.

Minka. My poor nerves are in a dreadful state.

Curdy. You made much more fuss than I did.

Minka. *My* ears were much worse.

Curdy. Ya, boys are braver than girls.

Minka. I'm not a girl, I'm a Princess.

And she stalked away, as if she had suddenly remembered it was beneath her dignity to eat out of the same plate as a *common* kitten. She was so huffed with Curdy that she came and rubbed against Mrs. Bell's ankles and purred to show that *she* was graciously restored to favour. When Curdy had finished the last scrap on his plate, he came and rubbed against her too. His cheerful nature was

always ready to forgive . . . and, unlike Minka, to forget. Mrs. Bell risked stooping down and stroking the top of his head. And Minka actually didn't protest. Was peace really in sight at last?

18

U P IN the study, both kittens had a nap, lying at opposite ends of the hearthrug. Mrs. Bell managed to get a little work done. Then just as she was in the middle of a sentence, she heard a terrific scuffling. She looked up and, to her alarm, saw a mixed bundle of cream and orange fur rolling about on the floor. Now a spiky striped tail would emerge from the bundle, now a brown kinky one; an orange boxing-glove would hold down a brown ear, a slim chocolate paw would buffet a flannel-pink nose. But there was no snarling and no claws were out. The next moment the bundle split in two and a slender half-grown cream kitten and a fat baby marmalade one were chasing each other madly all over the room. You never saw such a commotion: in and out and under and over the chairs they went; they plumped on to Mrs. Bell's desk and scattered the papers; they jumped over each other's backs and batted each other's tails. Minka ran up the curtains and Curdy tried to follow her and got stuck half-way. He dropped off and started playing on his own with the cork on the string. Minka, who hadn't played with this for weeks, leapt down from the top of the curtains and returned the cork to him smartly as it swung away. They had a fine rally which ended in Curdy's winding himself up in the string and having to be unwound by Mrs. Bell. Never had Mrs. Bell seen two kittens have a more glorious game. Minka had forgotten all about pretending to be a grown-up cat and was romping even more wildly than Curdy. It was he who gave up first and took refuge on a chair, for she was getting a little rough in her excitement, being bigger and stronger than he was. In a minute he was curled up, fast asleep. Minka went up and patted him

as if to say: 'Come on, lazybones.' Then suddenly she yawned, leapt up on the chair, and carefully draped herself round him. The next moment she too was fast asleep, with her cheek against his and one long brown-stockinged leg laid protectively over him. She might have been a tiny mother-cat cuddling a kitten much too big for her.

It so happened that Alice was not coming home after work that Monday, but spending the night with a friend. When bedtime came, Mrs. Bell was terribly puzzled what to do about Curdy. It seemed very hard to shut him up all alone, since he was used to company at night. On the other hand, her bedroom was sacred to Minka. Wonderfully as the two kittens had got on together all day, it was, after all, the first time that there had been more than brief moments of harmony. Suppose she spoilt everything by being tactless with Minka, just as Curdy was always doing? If there was one thing likely to rouse Minka's furious jealousy again, it would surely be to allow him to intrude on their private nights.

She decided to compromise. As Curdy was mercifully asleep already, she carried him into Alice's bedroom which was next door to hers and laid him on the bed. He yawned and gave a drowsy squeak, but, by the time she had brought his tray in, he was sound asleep. Then she propped Alice's bedroom door open, as she always did her own so that Minka could get out to her tray. If Curdy woke up and felt lonely, he could walk out of Alice's room . . . If he happened to walk into Mrs. Bell's . . . well, she'd just have to take the risk. Perhaps Minka would be asleep by then, anyhow.

Minka had her usual evening romp with Mrs. Bell as she undressed, making rushes at her toes, pulling the belt off her dressing-gown and having a mock battle with her empty shoes. But the moment Mrs. Bell was in bed,

Minka cuddled into her usual place on her left shoulder and began to purr so loudly it was almost like a gentle, rhythmical snore. But, just as Mrs. Bell put up her hand to turn off the bedside lamp, she heard a plaintive squeal. Round the door came a round, fluffy, pansy face, followed by a barrel of a body and a pointed tail carried like a flag. The next moment, Curdy had jumped up on the bed and was padding softly across Mrs. Bell's body. Mrs. Bell held her breath. No, it was all right. Minka was still purring. On came Curdy, stopping on Mrs. Bell's chest to do a little kneading with his big tufty paws, till he was so close that his whiskers tickled her face. Minka had not moved, but she had stopped purring. It was a tense moment.

Then suddenly Curdy side-stepped. He clawed back a piece of sheet and quietly inserted himself under it, nestling into Mrs. Bell's *right* shoulder . . . just as he had that first night in Rye. Still no sound from Minka, though Mrs. Bell felt her shift a little. In the silence she could hear Curdy's funny little wheezy purr that kept breaking off and restarting. Then all at once she felt Minka relax and settle again. There was one little sigh . . . and the deep, vibrating Siamese purr started up again. It completely drowned Curdy's feeble one but Mrs. Bell could still feel his body throbbing softly against her neck. Carefully, so as not to disturb either of them, she turned off the light.

She lay in the dark feeling wonderfully content.

Her dream had come true. Here she was, with her sun-kitten on one shoulder and her moon-kitten on the other,

peacefully purring *them*-selves and *her*self to sleep. And she knew that, though there would be occasional bickers and they would both sometimes tease her like mad, she and Curdy and Minka were going to be very happy indeed.

THE END

Also of Interest from Virago

FROST IN MAY
by Antonia White

'Intense, troubling, semi-miraculous – a work of art'
– Elizabeth Bowen

Nanda Gray, the daughter of a convert, is nine when, in 1908, she goes to the Convent of the Five Wounds; fourteen when, catastrophically, she leaves. Quick-witted and eager to please, Nanda is absorbed into a closed world and learns, with all the enthusiasm of the outsider, that her desires must be only those the Church permits. Here authority, self-control and rigid conformity hold sway, and passionate friendships form the only deviation from a rule which decrees obedience to be the highest goal. Daily life – the smell of beeswax in the corridors; the eccentricities of Nanda's friends, daughters of old European Catholic families – is caught to perfection as Nanda's downfall inexorably unfolds. This, Antonia White's most famous novel, is much more than a school story: it is a lyrical account of the death of a soul.

ANTONIA WHITE DIARIES 1926–1957
Edited by Susan Chitty

'These diaries, with their raw pain, uncertainty and wit, are a
powerful creative achievement . . . they illuminate a life that
was both an extreme and a paradigm of its time' – *Observer*

The first of two volumes of Antonia White's *Diaries* concentrates
on the years after the publication of *Frost in May* in 1933 and
moves through the completion of that famous Quartet over
twenty years later, to her contemplation of a fifth, unfinished
novel. An amalgam of confession, self-analysis and notebook,
their fluency is at odds with the writers' block that consistently
haunted the years she chronicles here. With breathtaking
honesty Antonia White also recounts the collapse of her third
marriage, her intense, troubled relationship with her daughters,
her desperate quest for love and her reconciliation with
Catholicism. These *Diaries* are an unparalleled record of a
writer's vision and life.

Antonia White's *Diaries 1958–1979* will be published by Virago
in March 1993.